DUE DATE

AUG – 8 1994			
	201-6503		Printed in USA

Modern Critical Interpretations

Marcel Proust's
Remembrance of Things Past

Modern Critical Interpretations

These and other titles in preparation

Modern Critical Interpretations

Marcel Proust's
Remembrance of Things Past

Edited and with an introduction by
Harold Bloom
Sterling Professor of the Humanities
Yale University

Chelsea House Publishers ◇ *1987*
NEW YORK ◇ NEW HAVEN ◇ PHILADELPHIA

© 1987 by Chelsea House Publishers,
a division of Chelsea House Educational Communications, Inc.,
  95 Madison Avenue, New York, NY 10016
  345 Whitney Avenue, New Haven, CT 06511
  5014 West Chester Pike, Edgemont, PA 19028

Introduction © 1987 by Harold Bloom

Printed and bound in the United States of America

∞ The paper used in this publication meets the minimum
requirements of the American National Standard for Permanence
of Paper for Printed Library Materials, Z39.48–1984.

Library of Congress Cataloging-in-Publication Data
Marcel Proust's Remembrance of things past.
  (Modern critical interpretations)
  Bibliography: p.
  Includes index.
  Summary: A collection of critical essays on Proust's "Remembrance
of Things Past" arranged in chronological order of publication.
  1. Proust, Marcel, 1871–1922. A la recherche du temps perdu.
[1. Proust, Marcel, 1871–1922. Remembrance of things past. 2. French
literature—History and criticism] I. Bloom, Harold. II. Series.
PQ2631.R63A832   1987   843'.912   86–29177
ISBN 1–55546–075–5   (alk. paper)

Contents

Editor's Note

This book brings together a representative selection of the best criticism available in English on Proust's *Remembrance of Things Past* (or *In Search of Lost Time*), universally regarded as the major Western novel of our century. The critical essays are reprinted here in the chronological order of their original publication. I am grateful to Kevin Pask for his assistance in editing this volume.

My introduction confines itself to Proust's extraordinary insights into sexual jealousy, as set forth throughout *Remembrance*. Samuel Beckett, at once the legitimate heir of Proust, Joyce, and Kafka, begins the chronological sequence with his powerful meditation upon the obsessive concerns that Proust shared with his precursor, Ruskin, and Ruskin with his own forerunner, Wordsworth. The German-Jewish critic Walter Benjamin isolates what for him was the image of Proust, while Georges Bataille, erudite in the morality of eroticism, applies his expert gaze to Proust's rather different moral universe.

René Girard, our modern authority upon mediated desire, extends his vision of that mode of deceit to *Remembrance*. The dialectic of structure and temporality in Proust, a much-debated matter, is investigated by Richard Macksey, while the complementary problem of Proustian space is described by the eminent critic of consciousness Georges Poulet. Very different from these approaches is the reading of Proust by the late Paul de Man, master of the deconstructive mode that examines the epistemology of rhetorical language.

De Man's influence is reflected in the remaining essays in this volume, and seems inescapable in any future readings of Proust. Richard Terdiman studies the question of narrative perspective in *Remembrance*, while David R. Ellison concludes this book with an advanced reading of the ways in which Proust makes highly problematical his own representation of his authorial self as "Marcel."

Introduction

Sexual jealousy is the most novelistic of circumstances, just as incest, according to Shelley, is the most poetical of circumstances. Proust is the novelist of our era, even as Freud is our moralist. Both are speculative thinkers, who divide between them the eminence of being the prime wisdom writers of the age.

Proust died in 1922, the year of Freud's grim and splendid essay, "Certain Neurotic Mechanisms in Jealousy, Paranoia, and Homosexuality." Both of them great ironists, tragic celebrants of the comic spirit, Proust and Freud are not much in agreement on jealousy, paranoia, and homosexuality, though both start with the realization that all of us are bisexual in nature.

Freud charmingly begins his essay by remarking that jealousy, like grief, is normal and comes in three stages: *competitive*, or normal, *projected, delusional*. The *competitive*, or garden variety, is compounded of grief, due to the loss of the loved object, and of the reactivation of the narcissistic scar, the tragic first loss, by the infant, of the parent of the other sex to the parent of the same sex. As normal, *competitive* jealousy is really normal Hell, Freud genially throws into the compound such delights as enmity against the successful rival, some self-blaming, self-criticism, and a generous portion of bisexuality.

Projected jealousy attributes to the erotic partner one's own actual unfaithfulness or repressed impulses, and is cheerfully regarded by Freud as being relatively innocuous, since its almost delusional character is highly amenable to analytic exposure of unconscious fantasies. But *delusional* jealousy proper is more serious; it also takes its origin in repressed impulses towards infidelity, but the object of those impulses is of one's own sex, and this, for Freud, moves one across the border into paranoia.

1

What the three stages of jealousy have in common is a bisexual component, since even *projected* jealousy trades in repressed impulses, and these include homosexual desires. Proust, our other authority on jealousy, preferred to call homosexuality "inversion," and in a brilliant mythological fantasia traced the sons of Sodom and the daughters of Gomorrah to the surviving exiles from the Cities of the Plain. Inversion and jealousy, so intimately related in Freud, become in Proust a dialectical pairing, with the aesthetic sensibility linked to both as a third term in a complex series.

On the topos of jealousy, Proust is fecund and generous; no writer has devoted himself so lovingly and brilliantly to expounding and illustrating the emotion, except of course Shakespeare in *Othello* and Hawthorne in *The Scarlet Letter*. Proust's jealous lovers—Swann, Saint-Loup, above all Marcel himself—suffer so intensely that we sometimes need to make an effort not to empathize too closely. It is difficult to determine just what Proust's stance towards their suffering is, partly because Proust's ironies are both pervasive and cunning. Comedy hovers nearby, but even tragicomedy seems an inadequate term for the compulsive sorrows of Proust's protagonists. Swann, after complimenting himself that he has not, by his jealousy, proved to Odette that he loves her too much, falls into the mouth of Hell:

> He never spoke to her of this misadventure, and ceased even to think of it himself. But now and then his thoughts in their wandering course would come upon this memory where it lay unobserved, would startle it into life, thrust it forward into his consciousness, and leave him aching with a sharp, deep-rooted pain. As though it were a bodily pain, Swann's mind was powerless to alleviate it; but at least, in the case of bodily pain, since it is independent of the mind, the mind can dwell upon it, can note that it has diminished, that it has momentarily ceased. But in this case the mind, merely by recalling the pain, created it afresh. To determine not to think of it was to think of it still, to suffer from it still. And when, in conversation with his friends, he forgot about it, suddenly a word casually uttered would make him change countenance like a wounded man when a clumsy hand has touched his aching limb. When he came away from Odette he was happy, he felt calm, he recalled her smiles, of gentle mockery when speaking of this or that other person, of

tenderness for himself; he recalled the gravity of her head which she seemed to have lifted from its axis to let it droop and fall, as though in spite of herself, upon his lips, as she had done on the first evening in the carriage, the languishing looks she had given him as she lay in his arms, nestling her head against her shoulder as though shrinking from the cold.

But then at once his jealousy, as though it were the shadow of his love, presented him with the complement, with the converse of that new smile with which she had greeted him that very evening—and which now, perversely, mocked Swann and shone with love for another—of that droop of the head, now sinking on to other lips, of all the marks of affection (now given to another) that she had shown to him. And all the voluptuous memories which he bore away from her house were, so to speak, but so many sketches, rough plans like those which a decorator submits to one, enabling Swann to form an idea of the various attitudes, aflame or faint with passion, which she might adopt for others. With the result that he came to regret every pleasure that he tasted in her company, every new caress of which he had been so imprudent as to point out to her the delights, every fresh charm that he found in her, for he knew that, a moment later, they would go to enrich the collection of instruments in his secret torture-chamber.

Jealousy here is a pain experienced by Freud's bodily ego, on the frontier between psyche and body: "To determine not to think of it was to think of it still, to suffer from it still." As the shadow of love, jealousy resembles the shadow cast by the earth up into the heavens, where by tradition it ought to end at the sphere of Venus. Instead, it darkens there, and since the shadow is Freud's reality principle, or our consciousness of our own mortality, Proust's dreadfully persuasive irony is that jealousy exposes not only the arbitrariness of every erotic object-choice but also marks the passage of the loved person into a teleological overdetermination, in which the supposed inevitability of the person is simply a mask for the inevitability of the lover's death. Proust's jealousy thus becomes peculiarly akin to Freud's death drive, since it, too, quests beyond the pleasure/unpleasure principle. Our secret torture-chamber is furnished anew by every recollection of the beloved's erotic prowess, since what delighted us has delighted others.

Swann experiences the terrible conversion of the jealous lover into a parody of the scholar, a conversion to an intellectual pleasure that is more a deviation than an achievement, since no thought can be emancipated from the sexual past of all thought (Freud), if the search for truth is nothing but a search for the sexual past:

> Certainly he suffered as he watched that light, in whose golden atmosphere, behind the closed sash, stirred the unseen and detested pair, as he listened to that murmur which revealed the presence of the man who had crept in after his own departure, the perfidy of Odette, and the pleasures which she was at that moment enjoying with the stranger. And yet he was not sorry he had come; the torment which had forced him to leave his own house had become less acute now that it had become less vague, now that Odette's other life, of which he had had, at that first moment, a sudden helpless suspicion, was definitely there, in the full glare of the lamp-light, almost within his grasp, an unwitting prisoner in that room into which, when he chose, he would force his way to seize it unawares; or rather he would knock on the shutters, as he often did when he came very late, and by that signal Odette would at least learn that he knew, that he had seen the light and had heard the voices, and he himself, who a moment ago had been picturing her as laughing with the other at his illusions, now it was he who saw them, confident in their error, tricked by none other than himself, whom they believed to be far away but who was there, in person, there with a plan, there with the knowledge that he was going, in another minute, to knock on the shutter. And perhaps the almost pleasurable sensation he felt at that moment was something more than the assuagement of a doubt, and of a pain: was an intellectual pleasure. If, since he had fallen in love, things had recovered a little of the delightful interest that they had had for him long ago—though only in so far as they were illuminated by the thought or the memory of Odette—now it was another of the faculties of his studious youth that his jealousy revived, the passion for truth, but for a truth which, too, was interposed between himself and his mistress, receiving its light from her alone, a private and personal truth the sole

object of which (an infinitely precious object, and one almost disinterested in its beauty) was Odette's life, her actions, her environment, her plans, her past. At every other period in his life, the little everyday activities of another person had always seemed meaningless to Swann; if gossip about such things was repeated to him, he would dismiss it as insignificant, and while he listened it was only the lowest, the most commonplace part of his mind that was engaged; these were the moments when he felt at his most inglorious. But in this strange phase of love the personality of another person becomes so enlarged, so deepened, that the curiosity which he now felt stirring inside him with regard to the smallest details of a woman's daily life, was the same thirst for knowledge with which he had once studied history. And all manner of actions from which hitherto he would have recoiled in shame, such as spying, to-night, outside a window, to-morrow perhaps, for all he knew, putting adroitly provocative questions to casual witnesses, bribing servants, listening at doors, seemed to him now to be precisely on a level with the deciphering of manuscripts, the weighing of evidence, the interpretation of old monuments—so many different methods of scientific investigation with a genuine intellectual value and legitimately employable in the search for truth.

In fact, poor Swann is at the wrong window, and the entire passage is therefore as exquisitely painful as it is comic. What Freud ironically called the overevaluation of the object, the enlargement or deepening of the beloved's personality, begins to work not as one of the enlargements of life (like Proust's own novel) but as the deepening of a personal Hell. Swann plunges downwards and outwards, as he leans "in impotent, blind, dizzy anguish over the bottomless abyss" and reconstructs the petty details of Odette's past life with "as much passion as the aesthete who ransacks the extant documents of fifteenth-century Florence in order to penetrate further into the soul of the Primavera, the fair Vanna or the Venus of Botticelli."

The historicizing aesthete, John Ruskin, say, or Walter Pater, becomes the archetype of the jealous lover, who searches into lost time not for a person, but for an epiphany or moment-of-moments, a privileged fiction of duration:

When he had been paying social calls Swann would often come home with little time to spare before dinner. At that point in the evening, around six o'clock, when in the old days he used to feel so wretched, he no longer asked himself what Odette might be about, and was hardly at all concerned to hear that she had people with her or had gone out. He recalled at times that he had once, years ago, tried to read through its envelope a letter addressed by Odette to Forcheville. But this memory was not pleasing to him, and rather than plumb the depths of shame that he felt in it he preferred to indulge in a little grimace, twisting up the corners of his mouth and adding, if need be, a shake of the head which signified "What do I care about it?" True, he considered now that the hypothesis on which he had often dwelt at that time, according to which it was his jealous imagination alone that blackened what was in reality the innocent life of Odette—that this hypothesis (which after all was beneficent, since, so long as his amorous malady had lasted, it had diminished his sufferings by making them seem imaginary) was not the correct one, that it was his jealousy that had seen things in the correct light, and that if Odette had loved him more than he supposed, she had also deceived him more. Formerly, while his sufferings were still keen, he had vowed that, as soon as he had ceased to love Odette and was no longer afraid either of vexing her or of making her believe that he loved her too much, he would give himself the satisfaction of elucidating with her, simply from his love of truth and as a point of historical interest, whether or not Forcheville had been in bed with her that day when he had rung her bell and rapped on her window in vain, and she had written to Forcheville that it was an uncle of hers who had called. But this so interesting problem, which he was only waiting for his jealousy to subside before clearing up, had precisely lost all interest in Swann's eyes when he had ceased to be jealous. Not immediately, however. Long after he had ceased to feel any jealousy with regard to Odette, the memory of that day, that afternoon spent knocking vainly at the little house in the Rue La Pérouse, had continued to torment him. It was as though his jealousy, not dissimilar in that respect from those maladies which appear to have their seat, their centre of contagion, less in certain persons than in certain places, in certain houses, had had for its object not so much Odette herself as that day, that hour in the irrevocable past when Swann had knocked at every entrance to her house in turn, as though that day, that hour alone had caught and preserved a few last fragments of the amorous personality which had once been Swann's, that there alone could he now recapture them. For a long time now it had been a matter of indifference to him whether Odette had been, or was being, unfaithful to him. And yet he had continued for some years to seek out old servants of hers, to such an extent had the painful curiosity persisted in him to know whether on that day, so long ago, at six o'clock, Odette had been in bed with Forcheville. Then that curiosity itself had disappeared, without, however, his abandoning his investigations. He went on trying to discover what no longer interested him, because his old self, though it had shrivelled to extreme decrepitude, still acted mechanically, in accordance with preoccupations so utterly abandoned that Swann could not now succeed even in picturing to himself that anguish—so compelling once that he had been unable to imagine that he would ever be delivered from it, that only the death of the woman he loved (though death, as will be shown later on in this story by a cruel corroboration, in no way diminishes the sufferings caused by jealousy) seemed to him capable of smoothing the path of his life which then seemed impassably obstructed.

Jealousy dies with love, but only with respect to the former beloved. Horribly a life-in-death, jealousy renews itself like the moon, perpetually trying to discover what no longer interests it, even after the object of desire has been literally buried. Its true object is "that day, that hour in the irrevocable past," and even that time was less an actual time than a temporal fiction, an episode in the evanescence of one's own self. Paul de Man's perspective that Proust's deepest insight is the nonexistence of the self founds itself upon this temporal irony of unweaving, this permanent parabasis of meaning. One can remember that even this deconstructive perspective is no more or less privileged than any other Proustian trope, and so cannot give us a truth that Proust himself evades.

II

The bridge between Swann's jealousy and Marcel's is Saint-Loup's jealousy of Rachel, summed up by Proust in one of his magnificently long, baroque paragraphs:

Saint-Loup's letter had come as no surprise to me, even though I had had no news of him since, at the time of my grandmother's illness, he had accused me of perfidy and treachery. I had grasped at once what must have happened. Rachel, who liked to provoke his jealousy (she also had other causes for resentment against me), had persuaded her lover that I had made sly attempts to have relations with her in his absence. It is probable that he continued to believe in the truth of this allegation, but he had ceased to be in love with her, which meant that its truth or falsehood had become a matter of complete indifference to him, and our friendship alone remained. When, on meeting him again, I tried to talk to him about his accusations, he merely gave me a benign and affectionate smile which seemed to be a sort of apology, and then changed the subject. All this was not to say that he did not, a little later, see Rachel occasionally when he was in Paris. Those who have played a big part in one's life very rarely disappear from it suddenly for good. They return to it at odd moments (so much so that people suspect a renewal of old love) before leaving it for ever. Saint-Loup's breach with Rachel had very soon become less painful to him, thanks to the soothing pleasure that was given him by her incessant demands for money. Jealousy, which prolongs the course of love, is not capable of containing many more ingredients than the other products of the imagination. If one takes with one, when one starts on a journey, three or four images which incidentally one is sure to lose on the way (such as the lilies and anemones heaped on the Ponte Vecchio, or the Persian church shrouded in mist), one's trunk is already pretty full. When one leaves a mistress, one would be just as glad, until one had begun to forget her, that she should not become the property of three or four potential protectors whom one pictures in one's mind's eye, of whom, that is to say, one is jealous: all those whom one does not so picture count for nothing. Now frequent demands for money from a cast-off mistress no more give one a complete idea of her life than charts showing a high temperature would of her illness. But the latter would at any rate be an indication that she was ill, and the former furnish a presumption, vague enough it is true, that the forsaken one or forsaker (whichever she be) cannot have found anything very remarkable in the way of rich protectors. And so each demand is welcomed with the joy which a lull produces in the jealous one's sufferings, and answered with the immediate dispatch of money, for naturally one does not like to think of her being in want of anything except lovers (one of the three lovers one has in one's mind's eye), until time has enabled one to regain one's composure and to learn one's successor's name without wilting. Sometimes Rachel came in so late at night that she could ask her former lover's permission to lie down beside him until the morning. This was a great comfort to Robert, for it reminded him how intimately, after all, they had lived to-together, simply to see that even if he took the greater part of the bed for himself it did not in the least interfere with her sleep. He realised that she was more comfortable, lying close to his familiar body, than she would have been elsewhere, that she felt herself by his side—even in an hotel—to be in a bedroom known of old in which one has one's habits, in which one sleeps better. He felt that his shoulders, his limbs, all of him, were for her, even when he was unduly restless from insomnia or thinking of the things he had to do, so entirely usual that they could not disturb her and that the perception of them added still further to her sense of repose.

The heart of this comes in the grandly ironic sentence: "Jealousy, which prolongs the course of love, is not capable of containing many more ingredients than the other products of the imagination." That is hardly a compliment to the capaciousness of the imagination, which scarcely can hold on for long to even three or four images. Saint-Loup, almost on the farthest shore of jealousy, has the obscure comfort of having become, for Rachel, one of those images not quite faded away, when "he felt that his shoulders, his limbs, all of him, were for her," even when he has ceased to be there, or anywhere, for her, or she for him. Outliving love, jealousy has become love's last stand, the final basis for a continuity between two former lovers.

Saint-Loup's bittersweet evanescence as a lover contrasts both with Swann's massive historicism and with the novel's triumphant representation of jealousy, Marcel's monumental search after lost time in the long aftermath of Albertine's death. Another grand link between magnificent jealousies is provided by Swann's observations to Marcel, aesthetic reflections somewhat removed from the pain of earlier realities:

> It occurred to me that Swann must be getting tired of waiting for me. Moreover I did not wish to be too late in returning home because of Albertine, and, taking leave of Mme de Surgis and M. de Charlus, I went in search of my invalid in the card-room. I asked him whether what he had said to the Prince in their conversation in the garden was really what M. de Bréauté (whom I did not name) had reported to us, about a little play by Bergotte. He burst out laughing: "There's not a word of truth in it, not one, it's a complete fabrication and would have been an utterly stupid thing to say. It's really incredible, this spontaneous generation of falsehood. I won't ask who it was that told you, but it would be really interesting, in a field as limited as this, to work back from one person to another and find out how the story arose. Anyhow, what concern can it be of other people, what the Prince said to me? People are very inquisitive. I've never been inquisitive, except when I was in love, and when I was jealous. And a lot I ever learned! Are you jealous?" I told Swann that I had never experienced jealousy, that I did not even know what it was. "Well, you can count yourself lucky. A little jealousy is not too unpleasant, for two reasons. In the first place, it enables people who are not inquisitive to take an interest in the lives of others, or of one other at any rate. And then it makes one feel the pleasure of possession, of getting into a carriage with a woman, of not allowing her to go about by herself. But that's only in the very first stages of the disease, or when the cure is almost complete. In between, it's the most agonising torment. However, I must confess that I haven't had much experience even of the two pleasures I've mentioned—the first because of my own nature, which is incapable of sustained reflexion; the second because of circumstances, because of the woman, I should say the women, of whom I've been jealous. But

that makes no difference. Even when one is no longer attached to things, it's still something to have been attached to
them; because it was always for reasons which other people
didn't grasp. The memory of those feelings is something
that's to be found only in ourselves; we must go back into
ourselves to look at it. You mustn't laugh at this idealistic
jargon, but what I mean to say is that I've been very fond of
life and very fond of art. Well, now that I'm a little too
weary to live with other people, those old feelings, so personal and individual, that I had in the past, seem to me—it's
the mania of all collectors—very precious. I open my heart
to myself like a sort of showcase, and examine one by one
all those love affairs of which the rest of the world can have
known nothing. And of this collection, to which I'm now
even more attached than to my others, I say to myself,
rather as Mazarin said of his books, but in fact without the
least distress, that it will be very tiresome to have to leave it
all. But, to come back to my conversation with the Prince, I
shall tell one person only, and that person is going to be
you."

We are in the elegy season, ironically balanced between the death
of jealousy in Swann and its birth in poor Marcel, who literally does
not know that the descent into Avernus beckons. When the vigor of an
affirmation has more power than its probability, clearly we are living
in a fiction, the metaphor or transference that we call love, and might
call jealousy. Into that metaphor, Marcel moves like a sleepwalker,
with his obsessions central to *The Captive* and insanely pervasive in
The Fugitive. A great passage in *The Captive,* which seems a diatribe
against jealousy, instead is a passionately ironic celebration of jealousy's aesthetic victory over our merely temporal happiness:

However, I was still at the first stage of enlightenment with
regard to Léa. I was not even aware whether Albertine knew
her. No matter, it came to the same thing. I must at all costs
prevent her from renewing this acquaintance or making the
acquaintance of this stranger at the Trocadéro. I say that I
did not know whether she knew Léa or not; yet I must in
fact have learned this at Balbec, from Albertine herself. For
amnesia obliterated from my mind as well as from Albertine's
a great many of the statements that she had made to me.

Memory, instead of being a duplicate, always present before
one's eyes, of the various events of one's life, is rather a void
from which at odd moments a chance resemblance enables
one to resuscitate dead recollections; but even then there are
innumerable little details which have not fallen into that
potential reservoir of memory, and which will remain forever unverifiable. One pays no attention to anything that
one does not connect with the real life of the woman one
loves; one forgets immediately what she has said to one
about such and such an incident or such and such people one
does not know, and her expression while she was saying it.
And so when, in due course, one's jealousy is aroused by
these same people, and seeks to ascertain whether or not it is
mistaken, whether it is indeed they who are responsible for
one's mistress's impatience to go out, and her annoyance
when one has prevented her from doing so by returning
earlier than usual, one's jealousy, ransacking the past in
search of a clue, can find nothing; always retrospective, it is
like a historian who has to write the history of a period for
which he has no documents; always belated, it dashes like an
enraged bull to the spot where it will not find the dazzling,
arrogant creature who is tormenting it and whom the crowd
admire for his splendour and cunning. Jealousy thrashes
around in the void, uncertain as we are in those dreams in
which we are distressed because we cannot find in his empty
house a person whom we have known well in life, but who
here perhaps is another person and has merely borrowed the
features of our friend, uncertain as we are even more after
we awake when we seek to identify this or that detail of our
dream. What was one's mistress's expression when she told
one that? Did she not look happy, was she not actually
whistling, a thing that she never does unless she has some
amorous thought in her mind and finds one's presence im-
portunate and irritating? Did she not tell one something that
is contradicted by what she now affirms, that she knows or
does not know such and such a person? One does not know,
and one will never know; one searches desperately among
the unsubstantial fragments of a dream, and all the time
one's life with one's mistress goes on, a life that is oblivious
of what may well be of importance to one, and attentive to

what is perhaps of none, a life hagridden by people who have no real connexion with one, full of lapses of memory, gaps, vain anxieties, a life as illusory as a dream.

Thrashing about in the void of a dream in which a good friend perhaps is another person, jealousy becomes Spenser's Malbecco: "who quite / Forgot he was a man, and jealousy is hight." Yet making life "as illusory as a dream," hagridden by lapses and gaps, is Marcel's accomplishment, and Proust's art. One does not write an other-than-ironic diatribe against one's own art. Proust warily, but with the sureness of a great beast descending upon its helpless prey, approaches the heart of his vision of jealousy, his sense that the emotion is akin to what Freud named as the defense of isolation, in which all context is burned away and a dangerous present replaces all past and all future.

Sexual jealousy in Proust is accompanied by a singular obsessiveness in regard to questions of space and of time. The jealous lover, who, as Proust says, conducts researches comparable to those of the scholar, seeks in his inquiries every detail he can find as to the location and duration of each betrayal and infidelity. Why? Proust has a marvelous passage in *The Fugitive* volume of *Remembrance*:

It is one of the faculties of jealousy to reveal to us the extent to which the reality of external facts and the sentiments of the heart are an unknown element which lends itself to endless suppositions. We imagine that we know exactly what things are and what people think, for the simple reason that we do not care about them. But as soon as we have a desire to know, as the jealous man has, then it becomes a dizzy kaleidoscope in which we can no longer distinguish anything. Had Albertine been unfaithful to me? With whom? In what house? On what day? On the day when she had said this or that to me, when I remembered that I had in the course of it said this or that? I could not tell. Nor did I know what her feelings were for me, whether they were inspired by self-interest or by affection. And all of a sudden I remembered some trivial incident, for instance that Albertine had wished to go to Saint-Martin-le-Vêtu, saying that the name interested her, and perhaps simply because she had made the acquaintance of some peasant girl who lived there. But it was useless that Aimé should have informed me of what he had learned from the woman at the baths, since

Albertine must remain eternally unaware that he had informed me, the need to know having always been exceeded, in my love for Albertine, by the need to show her that I knew; for this broke down the partition of different illusions that stood between us, without having ever had the result of making her love me more, far from it. And now, since she was dead, the second of these needs had been amalgamated with the effect of the first: the need to picture to myself the conversation in which I would have informed her of what I had learned, as vividly as the conversation in which I would have asked her to tell me what I did not know; that is to say, to see her by my side, to hear her answering me kindly, to see her cheeks become plump again, her eyes shed their malice and assume an air of melancholy; that is to say, to love her still and to forget the fury of my jealousy in the despair of my loneliness. The painful mystery of this impossibility of ever making known to her what I had learned and of establishing our relations upon the truth of what I had only just discovered (and would not have been able, perhaps, to discover but for her death) substituted its sadness for the more painful mystery of her conduct. What? To have so desperately desired that Albertine—who no longer existed—should know that I had heard the story of the baths! This again was one of the consequences of our inability, when we have to consider the fact of death, to picture to ourselves anything but life. Albertine no longer existed; but to me she was the person who had concealed from me that she had assignations with women at Balbec, who imagined that she had succeeded in keeping me in ignorance of them. When we try to consider what will happen to us after our own death, is it not still our living self which we mistakenly project at that moment? And is it much more absurd, when all is said, to regret that a woman who no longer exists is unaware that we have learned what she was doing six years ago than to desire that of ourselves, who will be dead, the public shall still speak with approval a century hence? If there is more real foundation in the latter than in the former case, the regrets of my retrospective jealousy proceeded none the less from the same optical error as in other men the desire for posthumous fame. And yet, if this impression of the solemn finality of my separation from Albertine had momentarily supplanted my idea of her misdeeds, it only succeeded in aggravating them by bestowing upon them an irremediable character. I saw myself astray in life as on an endless beach where I was alone and where, in whatever direction I might turn, I would never meet her.

"The regrets of my retrospective jealousy proceeded none the less from the same optical error as in other men the desire for posthumous fame"—is that not as much Proust's negative credo as it is Marcel's? Those "other men" include the indubitable precursors, Flaubert and Baudelaire, and Proust himself as well. The aesthetic agon for immortality is an optical error, yet this is one of those errors about life that are necessary for life, as Nietzsche remarked, and is also one of those errors about art that is art. Proust has swerved away from Flaubert into a radical confession of error; the novel is creative envy, love is jealousy, jealousy is the terrible fear that there will not be enough space for oneself (including literary space), and that there never can be enough time for oneself, because death is the reality of one's life. A friend once remarked to me, at the very height of her own jealousy, that jealousy was nothing but a vision of two bodies on a bed, neither of which was one's own, where the hurt resided in the realization that one body ought to have been one's own. Bitter as the remark may have been, it usefully reduces the trope of jealousy to literal fears: where was one's body, where will it be, when will it not be? Our ego is always a bodily ego, Freud insisted, and jealousy joins the bodily ego and the drive as another frontier concept, another vertigo whirling between a desperate inwardness and the injustice of outwardness. Proust, like Freud, goes back after all to the prophet Jeremiah, that uncomfortable sage who proclaimed a new inwardness for his mother's people. The law is written upon our inward parts for Proust also, and the law is justice, but the god of law is a jealous god, though he is certainly not the god of jealousy.

Freud, in "The Passing of the Oedipus Complex," writing two years after Proust's death, set forth a powerful speculation as to the difference between the sexes, a speculation that Proust neither evades nor supports, and yet illuminates, by working out of the world that Freud knows only in the pure good of theory. Freud is properly tentative, but also adroitly forceful:

Here our material—for some reason we do not understand —becomes far more shadowy and incomplete. The female sex develops an Oedipus-complex, too, a super-ego and a latency period. May one ascribe to it also a phallic organization and a castration complex? The answer is in the affirmative, but it cannot be the same as in the boy. The feministic demand for equal rights between the sexes does not carry far here; the morphological difference must express itself in differences in the development of the mind. "Anatomy is Destiny," to vary a saying of Napoleon's. The little girl's clitoris behaves at first just like a penis, but by comparing herself with a boy playfellow the child perceives that she has "come off short," and takes this fact as ill-treatment and as a reason for feeling inferior. For a time she still consoles herself with the expectation that later, when she grows up, she will acquire just as big an appendage as a boy. Here the woman's "masculine complex" branches off. The female child does not understand her actual loss as a sex characteristic, but explains it by assuming that at some earlier date she had possessed a member which was just as big and which had later been lost by castration. She does not seem to extend this conclusion about herself to other grown women, but in complete accordance with the phallic phase she ascribes to them large and complete, that is, male, genitalia. The result is an essential difference between her and the boy, namely, that she accepts castration as an established fact, an operation already performed, whereas the boy dreads the possibility of its being performed.

The castration-dread being thus excluded in her case, there falls away a powerful motive towards forming the super-ego and breaking up the infantile genital organization. These changes seem to be due in the girl far more than in the boy to the results of educative influences, of external intimidation threatening the loss of love. The Oedipus-complex in the girl is far simpler, less equivocal, than that of the little possessor of a penis; in my experience it seldom goes beyond the wish to take the mother's place, the feminine attitude towards the father. Acceptance of the loss of a penis is not endured without some attempt at compensation. The girl passes over—by way of a symbolic analogy, one may say—from the penis to a child; her Oedipus-complex culminates in the desire, which is long cherished, to be given a child by her father as a present, to bear him a child. One has the impression that the Oedipus-complex is later gradually abandoned because this wish is never fulfilled. The two desires, to possess a penis and to bear a child, remain powerfully charged with libido in the unconscious and help to prepare the woman's nature for its subsequent sex rôle. The comparative weakness of the sadistic component of the sexual instinct, which may probably be related to the penis-deficiency, facilitates the transformation of directly sexual trends into those inhibited in aim, feelings of tenderness. It must be confessed, however, that on the whole our insight into these processes of development in the girl is unsatisfying, shadowy and incomplete.

Anatomy is destiny in Proust also, but this is anatomy taken up into the mind, as it were. The exiles of Sodom and Gomorrah, more jealous even than other mortals, become monsters of time, yet heroes and heroines of time also. The Oedipus complex never quite passes, in Freud's sense of passing, either in Proust or in his major figures. Freud's castration complex, ultimately the dread of dying, is a metaphor for the same shadowed desire that Proust represents by the complex metaphor of jealousy. The jealous lover fears that he has been castrated, that his place in life has been taken, that true time is over for him. His only recourse is to search for lost time, in the hopeless hope that the aesthetic recovery of illusion and of experience alike, will deceive him in a higher mode than he fears to have been deceived in already.

Memory, Habit, Time

Samuel Beckett

The Proustian equation is never simple. The unknown, choosing its weapons from a hoard of values, is also the unknowable. And the quality of its action falls under two signatures. In Proust each spear may be a spear of Telephus. This dualism in multiplicity will be examined more closely in relation to Proust's "perspectivism." For the purposes of this synthesis it is convenient to adopt the *inner* chronology of the Proustian demonstration, and to examine in the first place that double-headed monster of damnation and salvation— Time.

The scaffolding of his structure is revealed to the narrator in the library of the Princesse de Guermantes (onetime Mme. Verdurin), and the nature of its materials in the matinée that follows. His book takes form in his mind. He is aware of the many concessions required of the literary artist by the shortcomings of the literary convention. As a writer he is not altogether at liberty to detach effect from cause. It will be necessary, for example, to interrupt (disfigure) the luminous projection of subject desire with the comic relief of features. It will be impossible to prepare the hundreds of masks that rightly belong to the objects of even his most disinterested scrutiny. He accepts regretfully the sacred ruler and compass of literary geometry. But he will refuse to extend his submission to spatial scales, he will refuse to measure the length and weight of man in terms of his body instead of in terms of his years. In the closing words of his book he states his position:

From *Proust*. © 1957 by Samuel Beckett. Grove Press, 1970.

But were I granted time to accomplish my work, I would not fail to stamp it with the seal of that Time, now so forcibly present to my mind, and in it I would describe men, even at the risk of giving them the appearance of monstrous beings, as occupying in Time a much greater place than that so sparingly conceded to them in Space, a place indeed extended beyond measure, because, like giants plunged in the years, they touch at once those periods of their lives—separated by so many days—so far apart in Time.

Proust's creatures, then, are victims of this predominating condition and circumstance—Time; victims as lower organisms, conscious only of two dimensions and suddenly confronted with the mystery of height, are victims: victims and prisoners. There is no escape from the hours and the days. Neither from tomorrow nor from yesterday. There is no escape from yesterday because yesterday has deformed us, or been deformed by us. The mood is of no importance. Deformation has taken place. Yesterday is not a milestone that has been passed, but a daystone on the beaten track of the years, and irremediably part of us, within us, heavy and dangerous. We are not merely more weary because of yesterday, we are other, no longer what we were before the calamity of yesterday. A calamitous day, but calamitous not necessarily in content. The good or evil disposition of the object has neither reality nor significance. The immediate joys and sorrows of the body and the intelligence are so many superfoetations. Such as it was, it has been assimilated to the only world that has reality and significance, the world of our own latent consciousness, and its cosmography has suffered a dislocation. So that we are rather in the position of Tantalus, with this difference, that we allow ourselves to be tantalised. And possibly the perpetuum mobile of our disillusions is subject to more variety. The aspirations of yesterday were valid for yesterday's ego, not for today's. We are disappointed at the nullity of what we are pleased to call attainment. But what is attainment? The identification of the subject with the object of his desire. The subject has died—and perhaps many times—on the way. For subject B to be disappointed by the banality of an object chosen by subject A is as illogical as to expect one's hunger to be dissipated by the spectacle of Uncle eating his dinner. Even suppose that by one of those rare miracles of coincidence, when the calendar of facts runs parallel to the calendar of feelings, realisation takes place, that the object of desire (in the strictest sense of that malady) is achieved by the subject, then the congruence is so perfect, the time-state of attainment eliminates so accurately the time-state of aspiration, that the actual seems the inevitable, and, all conscious intellectual effort to reconstitute the invisible and unthinkable as a reality being fruitless, we are incapable of appreciating our joy by comparing it with our sorrow. Voluntary memory (Proust repeats it ad nauseam) is of no value as an instrument of evocation, and provides an image as far removed from the real as the myth of our imagination or the caricature furnished by direct perception. There is only one real impression and one adequate mode of evocation. Over neither have we the least control. That reality and that mode will be discussed in their proper place.

But the poisonous ingenuity of Time in the science of affliction is not limited to its action on the subject, that action, as has been shown, resulting in an unceasing modification of his personality, whose permanent reality, if any, can only be apprehended as a retrospective hypothesis. The individual is the seat of a constant process of decantation, decantation from the vessel containing the fluid of future time, sluggish, pale and monochrome, to the vessel containing the fluid of past time, agitated and multicoloured by the phenomena of its hours. Generally speaking, the former is innocuous, amorphous, without character, without any Borgian virtue. Lazily considered in anticipation and in the haze of our smug will to live, of our pernicious and incurable optimism, it seems exempt from the bitterness of fatality: in store for us, not in store in us. On occasions, however, it is capable of supplementing the labours of its colleague. It is only necessary for its surface to be broken by a date, by any temporal specification allowing us to measure the days that separate us from a menace—or a promise. Swann, for example, contemplates with doleful resignation the months that he must spend away from Odette during the summer. One day Odette says: "Forcheville (her lover, and, after the death of Swann, her husband) is going to Egypt at Pentecost." Swann translates: "I am going with Forcheville to Egypt at Pentecost." The fluid of future time freezes, and poor Swann, face to face with the *future* reality of Odette and Forcheville in Egypt, suffers more grievously than even at the misery of his present condition. The narrator's desire to see La Berma in *Phèdre* is stimulated more violently by the announcement "Doors closed at two o'clock" than by the mystery of Bergotte's "Jansenist pallor and solar myth." His indifference at parting from Albertine at the end of the day in Balbec is transformed into the most horrible anxiety by a simple remark addressed by her to her aunt or to a friend: "Tomorrow, then, at half-past eight." The tacit understanding that the future can be controlled is destroyed. The future event cannot be focussed, its implications cannot be seized, until it is definitely situated and a date assigned to it. When Albertine was his prisoner, the possibility of her escape did not seriously disturb him, because it was indistinct and abstract, like the possibility of death. Whatever opinion we may be pleased to hold on the subject of death, we may be sure that it is meaningless and valueless. Death has not required us to keep a day free. The art of publicity has been revolutionised by a similar consideration. Thus I am exhorted, not merely to try the aperient of the Shepherd, but to try it at seven o'clock.

So far we have considered a mobile subject before an ideal object, immutable and incorruptible. But our vulgar perception is not concerned with other than vulgar phenomena. Exemption from intrinsic flux in a given object does not change the fact that it is the correlative of a subject that does not enjoy such immunity. The observer infects the observed with his own mobility. Moreover, when it is a case of human intercourse, we are faced by the problem of an object whose mobility is not merely a function of the subject's, but independent and personal: two separate and immanent dynamisms related by no system of synchronisation. So that whatever the object, our thirst for possession is, by definition, insatiable. At the best, all that is realised in Time (all Time produces), whether in Art or Life, can only be possessed successively, by a series of partial annexations—and never integrally and at once. The tragedy of the Marcel-Albertine liaison is the type-tragedy of the human relationship whose failure is preordained. My analysis of that central catastrophe will clarify this too abstract and arbitrary statement of Proust's pessimism. But for every tumour a scalpel and a compress. Memory and Habit are attributes of the Time cancer. They control the most simple Proustian episode, and an understanding of their mechanism must precede any particular analysis of their application. They are the flying buttresses of the temple raised to commemorate the wisdom of the architect that is also the wisdom of all the sages, from Brahma to Leopardi, the wisdom that consists not in the satisfaction but in the ablation of desire:

> "In noi di cari inganni
> non che la speme, il desiderio è spento."

The laws of memory are subject to the more general laws of habit. Habit is a compromise effected between the individual and his environment, or between the individual and his own organic eccentricities, the guarantee of a dull inviolability, the lightning-conductor of his existence. Habit is the ballast that chains the dog to his vomit. Breathing is habit. Life is habit. Or rather life is a succession of habits, since the individual is a succession of individuals; the world being a projection of the individual's consciousness (an objectivation of the individual's will, Schopenhauer would say), the pact must be continually renewed, the letter of safe-conduct brought up to date. The creation of the world did not take place once and for all time, but takes place every day. Habit then is the generic term for the countless treaties concluded between the countless subjects that constitute the individual and their countless correlative objects. The periods of transition that separate consecutive adaptations (because by no expedient of macabre transubstantiation can the grave-sheets serve as swaddling-clothes) represent the perilous zones in the life of the individual, dangerous, precarious, painful, mysterious and fertile, when for a moment the boredom of living is replaced by the suffering of being. (At this point, and with a heavy heart and for the satisfaction or disgruntlement of Gideans, semi and integral, I am inspired to concede a brief parenthesis to all the analogivorous, who are capable of interpreting the "Live dangerously," that victorious hiccough in vacuo, as the national anthem of the true ego exiled in habit. The Gideans advocate a habit of living—and look for an epithet. A nonsensical bastard phrase. They imply a hierarchy of habits, as though it were valid to speak of good habits and bad habits. An automatic adjustment of the human organism to the conditions of its existence has as little moral significance as the casting of a clout when May is or is not out; and the exhortation to cultivate a habit as little sense as an exhortation to cultivate a coryza.) The suffering of being: that is, the free play of every faculty. Because the pernicious devotion of habit paralyses our attention, drugs those handmaidens of perception whose co-operation is not absolutely essential. Habit is like Françoise, the immortal cook of the Proust household, who knows what has to be done, and will slave all day and all night rather than tolerate any redundant activity in the kitchen. But our current habit of living is as incapable of dealing with the mystery of a strange sky or a strange room, with any circumstance unforeseen in her curriculum, as Françoise of conceiving or realising the full horror of a Duval omelette. Then the atrophied faculties come to the rescue, and the maximum value of our being is restored. But less drastic circumstances may produce this tense and provisional lucidity in the nervous system. Habit may not be dead (or as good as dead, doomed to die) but sleeping. This second and more fugitive experience may or may not be exempt from pain. It does not inaugurate a period of transition. But the first and major mode is inseparable from suffering and anxiety—the suffering of the dying and the jealous anxiety of the ousted. The old ego dies hard. Such as it was, a minister of dulness, it was also an agent of security. When it ceases to perform that second function, when it is opposed by a phenomenon that it cannot reduce to the condition of a comfortable and familiar concept, when, in a word, it betrays its trust as a screen to spare its victim the spectacle of reality, it disappears, and the victim, now an ex-victim, for a moment free, is exposed to that reality—an exposure that has its advantages and its disadvantages. It disappears—with wailing and gnashing of teeth. The mortal microcosm cannot forgive the relative immortality of the macrocosm. The whisky bears a grudge against the decanter. The narrator cannot sleep in a strange room, is tortured by a high ceiling, being used to a low ceiling. What is taking place? The old pact is out of date. It contained no clause treating of high ceilings. The habit of friendship for the low ceiling is ineffectual, must die in order that a habit of friendship for the high ceiling may be born. Between this death and that birth, reality, intolerable, absorbed feverishly by his consciousness at the extreme limit of its intensity, by his total consciousness organised to avert the disaster, to create the new habit that will empty the mystery of its threat—and also of its beauty. "If Habit," writes Proust, "is a second nature, it keeps us in ignorance of the first, and is free of its cruelties and its enchantments." Our first nature, therefore, corresponding, as we shall see later, to a deeper instinct than the mere animal instinct of self-preservation, is laid bare during these periods of abandonment. And its cruelties and enchantments are the cruelties and enchantments of reality. "Enchantments of reality" has the air of a paradox. But when the object is perceived as particular and unique and not merely the member of a family, when it appears independent of any general notion and detached from the sanity of a cause, isolated and inexplicable in the light of ignorance, then and then only may it be a source of enchantment. Unfortunately Habit has laid its veto on this form of perception, its action being precisely to hide the essence—the Idea—of the object in the haze of conception—preconception. Normally we are in the position of the tourist (the traditional specification would constitute a pleonasm), whose aesthetic experience consists in a series of identifications and for whom Baedeker is the end rather than the means. Deprived by nature of the faculty of cognition and by upbringing of any acquaintance with the laws of dynamics, a brief inscription immortalises his emotion. The creature of habit turns aside from the object that cannot be made to correspond with one or other of his intellectual prejudices, that resists the propositions of his team of syntheses, organised by Habit on labour-saving principles.

Examples of these two modes—the death of Habit and the brief suspension of its vigilance—abound in Proust. I will transcribe two incidents in the life of the narrator. Of these the first, illustrative of the pact renewed, is extremely important as preparing a later incident that I will have occasion to discuss in relation to Proustian memory and Proustian revelation. The second exemplifies the pact waived in the interests of the narrator's via dolorosa.

The narrator arrives at Balbec-Plage, a holiday resort in Normandy, for the first time, accompanied by his grandmother. They are staying at the Grand Hotel. He enters his room, feverish and exhausted after his journey. But sleep, in this inferno of unfamiliar objects, is out of the question. All his faculties are on the alert, on the defensive, vigilant and taut, and as painfully incapable of relaxation as the tortured body of La Balue in his cage, where he could neither stand upright nor sit down. There is no room for his body in this vast and hideous apartment, because his attention has peopled it with gigantic furniture, a storm of sound and an agony of colour. Habit has not had time to silence the explosions of the clock, reduce the hostility of the violet curtains, remove the furniture and lower the inaccessible vault of this belvedere. Alone in this room that is not yet a room but a cavern of wild beasts, invested on all sides by the implacable strangers whose privacy he has disturbed, he desires to die. His grandmother comes in, comforts him, checks the stooping gesture that he makes to unbutton his boots, insists on helping him to undress, puts him to bed, and before leaving him makes him promise to knock on the partition that separates her room from his, should he require anything during the night. He knocks, and she comes again to him. But that night and for many nights he suffered. That suffering he interprets as the obscure, organic, humble refusal on the part of those elements that represented all that was best in his life to accept the possibility of a formula in which they would have no part. This reluctance to die, this long and desperate and daily resistance before the perpetual exfoliation of personality, explains also his horror at the idea of ever living without Gilberte Swann, of ever losing his parents, at the idea of his own death. But this terror at the thought of separation—from Gilberte, from his parents, from himself—is dissipated in a greater terror, when he thinks that to the pain of separation will succeed indifference, that the privation will cease to be a privation when the alchemy of Habit has transformed the individual capable of suffering into a stranger for whom the motives of that suffering are an idle tale, when not only the objects of his affection have vanished, but also that affection itself; and he thinks how absurd is our dream of a Paradise with retention of personality, since our life is a succession of Paradises successively denied, that the only true Paradise is the Paradise that has been lost, and that death will cure many of the desire for immortality.

The second episode that I have chosen as an illustration of the pact waived engages the same two characters, the narrator and his grandmother. He has been staying at Doncières with his friend Saint-Loup. He telephones to his grandmother in Paris. (After reading the description of this telephone call and its hardly less powerful corollary, when, years later, he speaks over the telephone with Albertine on returning home late after his first visit to the Princesse de Guermantes, Cocteau's *Voix Humaine* seems not merely a banality but an unnecessary banality.) After the conventional misunderstanding with the Vigilant Virgins (*sic*) of the central exchange, he hears his grandmother's voice, or what he assumes to be her voice, because he hears it now for the first time, in all its purity and reality, so different from the voice that he had been accustomed to follow on the open score of her face that he does not recognise it as hers. It is a grievous voice, its fragility unmitigated and undisguised by the carefully arranged mask of her features, and this strange real voice is the measure of its owner's suffering. He hears it also as the symbol of her isolation, of their separation, as impalpable as a voice from the dead. The voice stops. His grandmother seems as irretrievably lost as Eurydice among the shades. Alone before the mouthpiece he calls her name in vain. Nothing can persuade him to remain at Doncières. He must see his grandmother. He leaves for Paris. He surprises her reading her beloved Mme. de Sévigné. But he is not there because she does not know that he is there. He is present at his own absence. And, in consequence of his journey and his anxiety, his habit is in abeyance, the habit of his tenderness for his grandmother. His gaze is no longer the necromancy that sees in each precious object a mirror of the past. The notion of what he should see has not had time to interfere its prism between the eye and its object. His eye functions with the cruel precision of a camera; it photographs the reality of his grandmother. And he realises with horror that his grandmother is dead, long since and many times, that the cherished familiar of his mind, mercifully composed all along the years by the solicitude of habitual memory, exists no longer, that this mad old woman, drowsing over her book, overburdened with years, flushed and coarse and vulgar, is a stranger whom he has never seen.

The respite is brief. "Of all human plants," writes Proust, "Habit requires the least fostering, and is the first to appear on the seeming desolation of the most barren rock." Brief, and dangerously painful. The fundamental duty of Habit, about which it describes the futile and stupefying arabesques of its supererogations, consists in a perpetual adjustment and readjustment of our organic sensibility to the conditions of its worlds. Suffering represents the omission of that duty, whether through negligence or inefficiency, and boredom its adequate performance. The pendulum oscillates between these two terms: Suffering—that opens a window on the real and is the main condition of the artistic experience, and Boredom—with its host of top-hatted and hygienic ministers, Boredom that must be considered as the most tolerable because the most durable of human evils. Considered as a progression, this endless series of renovations leaves us as indifferent as the heterogeneity of any one of its terms, and the inconsequence of any given me disturbs us as little as the comedy of substitution. Indeed, we take as little cognisance of one as of the other, unless, vaguely, after the event, or clearly, when, as in the case of Proust, two birds in the bush are of infinitely greater value than one in the hand, and because—if I may add this nox vomica to an apéritif of metaphors—the heart of the cauliflower or the ideal core of the onion would represent a more appropriate tribute to the labours of poetical excavation than the crown of bay. I draw the conclusion of this matter from Proust's treasury of nutshell phrases: "If there were no such thing as Habit, Life would of necessity appear delicious to all those whom Death would threaten at every moment, that is to say, to all Mankind."

Proust had a bad memory—as he had an inefficient habit, because he had an inefficient habit. The man with a good memory does not remember anything because he does not forget anything. His memory is uniform, a creature of routine, at once a condition and function of his impeccable habit, an instrument of reference instead of an instrument of discovery. The pæan of his memory "I remember as well as I remember yesterday" is also its epitaph, and gives the precise expression of its value. He cannot *remember* yesterday any more than he can remember tomorrow. He can contemplate yesterday hung out to dry with the wettest August bank holiday on record a little further down the clothesline. Because his memory is a clothesline and the images of his past dirty linen redeemed and the infallibly complacent servants of his reminiscential needs. Memory is obviously conditioned by perception. Curiosity is a nonconditioned reflex, in its most primitive manifestations a reaction before a danger stimulus, and seldom exempt, even in its superior and apparently most disinterested form, from utilitarian considerations. Curiosity is the hair of our habit tending to stand on end. It rarely happens that our attention is not stained in greater or lesser degree by this animal element. Curiosity is the safeguard, not the death, of the cat, whether in skirts or on all fours. The more interested our interest, the more indelible must be its record of impressions. Its booty will always be available, because its aggression was a form of self-defence, i.e., the function of an invariable. In extreme cases memory is so closely related to habit that its word takes flesh, and is not merely available in cases of urgency, but habitually enforced. Thus absence of mind is fortunately compatible with the active presence of our organs of articulation. I repeat that rememoration, in its highest sense, cannot be applied to these extracts of our anxiety. Strictly speaking, we can only remember what has been registered by our extreme inattention and stored in that ultimate and inaccessible dungeon of our being to which Habit does not possess the key, and does not need to, because it contains none of the hideous and useful paraphernalia of war. But here, in that *gouffre interdit à nos sondes,* is stored the essence of ourselves, the best of our many selves and their concretions that simplists call the world, the best because accumulated slyly and painfully and patiently under the nose of our vulgarity, the fine essence of a smothered divinity whose whispered *disfazione* is drowned in the healthy bawling of an all-embracing appetite, the pearl that may give the lie to our carapace of paste and pewter. May—when we escape into the spacious annexe of mental alienation, in sleep or the rare dispensation of waking madness. From this deep source Proust hoisted his world. His work is not an accident, but its salvage is an accident. The conditions of that accident will be revealed at the peak of this prevision. A second-hand climax is better than none. But no purpose can be served by withholding the name of the diver. Proust calls him "involuntary memory." The memory that is not memory, but the application of a concordance to the Old Testament of the individual, he calls "voluntary memory." This is the uniform memory of intelligence; and it can be relied on to reproduce for our gratified inspection those impressions of the past that were consciously and intelligently formed. It has no interest in the mysterious element of inattention that colours our most commonplace experiences. It presents the past in monochrome. The images it chooses are as arbitrary as those chosen by imagination, and are equally remote from reality. Its action has been compared by Proust to that of turning the leaves of an album of photographs. The material that it furnishes contains nothing of the past, merely a blurred and uniform projection once removed of our anxiety and opportunism—that is to say, nothing. There is no great difference, says Proust, between the memory of a dream and the memory of reality. When the sleeper awakes, this emissary of his habit assures him that his "personality" has not disappeared with his fatigue. It is possible (for those that take an interest in such speculations) to consider the resurrection of the soul as a final piece of impertinence from the same source. It insists on that most necessary, wholesome and monotonous plagiarism—the plagiarism of oneself. This thoroughgoing democrat makes no distinction between the *Pensées* of Pascal and a soap advertisement. In fact, if Habit is the Goddess of Dulness, voluntary memory is Shadwell, and of Irish extraction. Involuntary memory is explosive, "an immediate, total and delicious deflagration." It restores, not merely the past object, but the Lazarus that it charmed or tortured, not merely Lazarus and the object, but more because less, more because it abstracts the useful, the opportune, the accidental, because in its flame it has consumed Habit and all its works, and in its brightness revealed what the mock reality of experience never can and never will reveal—the real. But involuntary memory is an unruly magician and will not be importuned. It chooses its own time and place for the performance of its miracle. I do not know how often this miracle recurs in Proust. I think twelve or thirteen times. But the first—the famous episode of the madeleine steeped in tea—would justify the assertion that his entire book is a monument to involuntary memory and the epic of its action. The whole of Proust's world comes out of a teacup, and not merely Combray and his childhood. For Combray brings us to the two "ways" and to Swann, and to Swann may be related every element of the Proustian experience and consequently its climax in revelation. Swann is behind Balbec,

and Balbec is Albertine and Saint-Loup. Directly he involves Odette
and Gilberte, the Verdurins and their clan, the music of Vinteuil and
the magical prose of Bergotte; indirectly (via Balbec and Saint-Loup)
the Guermantes, Oriane and the Duke, the Princesse and M. de Charlus.
Swann is the cornerstone of the entire structure, and the central figure
of the narrator's childhood, a childhood that involuntary memory,
stimulated or charmed by the long-forgotten taste of a madeleine steeped
in an infusion of tea, conjures in all the relief and colour of its essential
significance from the shallow well of a cup's inscrutable banality.

From this Janal, trinal, agile monster of Divinity: Time—a condition of resurrection because an instrument of death; Habit—an inflic-
tion in so far as it opposes the dangerous exaltation of the one and a
blessing in so far as it palliates the cruelty of the other; Memory—a
clinical laboratory stocked with poison and remedy, stimulant and
sedative: from Him the mind turns to the one compensation and
miracle of evasion tolerated by His tyranny and vigilance. This accidental and fugitive salvation in the midst of life may supervene when
the action of involuntary memory is stimulated by the negligence or
agony of Habit, and under no other circumstances, nor necessarily
then. Proust has adopted this mystic experience as the Leitmotiv of his
composition. It recurs, like the red phrase of the Vinteuil Septuor, a
neuralgia rather than a theme, persistent and monotonous, disappears
beneath the surface and emerges a still finer and more nervous structure, enriched with a strange and necessary incrustation of grace-notes,
a more confident and essential statement of reality, and climbs through
a series of precisions and purifications to the pinnacle from which it
commands and clarifies the most humble incident of its ascent and
delivers its triumphant ultimatum. It appears for the first time as the
episode of the madeleine, and again on at least five capital occasions
before its final and multiple investment of the Guermantes Hotel at the
opening of the second volume of *Le Temps retrouvé*, its culminating
and integral expression. Thus the germ of the Proustian solution is
contained in the statement of the problem itself. The source and point
of departure of this "sacred action," the elements of communion, are
provided by the physical world, by some immediate and fortuitous act
of perception. The process is almost one of intellectualised animism.
The following is the list of fetishes:

1. The madeleine steeped in an infusion of tea.

(Du côté de chez Swann)

2. The steeples of Martinville, seen from Dr. Percepied's
   trap.   *(Ibid.)*
3. A musty smell in a public lavatory in the Champs
   Elysées.
                        (A l'ombre des jeunes filles en fleurs)
4. The three trees, seen near Balbec from the carriage of
   Mme. de Villeparisis.   *(Ibid.)*
5. The hedge of hawthorn near Balbec.   *(Ibid.)*
6. He stoops to unbutton his boots on the occasion of his
   second visit to the Grand Hotel at Balbec.
                                       (Sodome et Gomorrhe)
7. Uneven cobbles in the courtyard of the Guermantes
   Hotel.   *(Le Temps retrouvé)*
8. The noise of a spoon against a plate.   *(Ibid.)*
9. He wipes his mouth with a napkin.   *(Ibid.)*
10. The noise of water in the pipes.   *(Ibid.)*
11. George Sand's *François le Champi*.   *(Ibid.)*

The list is not complete. I have not included a number of tentative
and abortive experiences, no one of which constitutes properly a recur-
rence of the motif, but rather a premonition of its approach. Of these
shadowy, incomplete evocations a certain cluster of three is specially
significant (*Côté de Guermantes*, 2, 80–82). He is waiting at home for
Mlle. de Stermaria (who might have been the narrator's Albertine if
she had not failed him then). He is transported successively to Balbec,
Doncières and Combray by the twilight perceived above the curtains
of his window, the descent of the stairs side by side with Robert de
Saint-Loup who has just arrived, and the dense fog that has settled on
the street. These three evocations, although incomplete, are intensely
violent, and for a moment he is conscious of the heterogeneous matter
and substance of these periods of his past: of the sombre, rugged
standstone of Combray, as opposed to the compact, glittering, translu-
cid, rose-veined alabaster of Rivebelle. But he is not alone, he is inter-
rupted by Saint-Loup, and what might have been the turning-point in
his life, the climax that is not to be reached until many years later in
the courtyard and library of the Princesse de Guermantes, is nothing
more than one of its most fugitive precursors.

The last five visitations—cobbles, spoon and plate, napkin, water
in the pipes, and *François le Champi*—may be considered as forming a
single annunciation and as providing the key to his life and work. The

sixth capital experience is particularly important (although less familiar than the famous madeleine, which is invariably quoted as the type of the Proustian revelation) as representing not only a central appearance of the motif but also an application of the erratic machinery of habit and memory as conceived by Proust. Albertine and the Proustian *Discours de la méthode* having waited so long can wait a little longer, and the reader is cordially invited to omit this summary analysis of what is perhaps the greatest passage that Proust ever wrote—*Les Intermittences du cœur.*

This incident takes place on the first evening of the narrator's second visit to Balbec. On this occasion he is with his mother, his grandmother having died a year before. But the dead annex the quick as surely as the Kingdom of France annexes the Duchy of Orléans. His mother has become his grandmother, whether through the suggestion of regret or an idolatrous cult of the dead or the disintegrating effect of loss that breaks the chrysalis and hastens the metamorphosis of an atavistic embryon whose maturation is slow and imperceptible without the stimulus of grief. She carries her mother's bag and her muff, and is never without a volume of Mme. de Sévigné. She who formerly chaffed her mother for never writing a letter without quoting Mme. de Sévigné or Mme. de Beausergent, builds now her own to her son around some phrase from the Letters or the Memoirs. The narrator's motives for this second visit are not those—furnished by Swann and his fantasy—that granted him no peace while Balbec had still the mystery and beauty of its name, before reality had replaced the mirage of imagination by the mirage of memory and explained away the value of the unknown as Venice will in due course be explained away and the odyssey of the local "tacot" through a mythical land by the etymology of Brichot and the appeasing contempt of familiarity. The Persian church with its stained glass "surfed in spray" and its steeple hewn out of the granite rampart of a Norman cliff has been replaced by the Giorgionesque chambermaid of Mme. de Putbus.

He arrives tired and ill, as on the former occasion that has been analysed as an example of the death of Habit. Now, however, the dragon has been reduced to docility, and the cavern is a room. Habit has been reorganised—an operation described by Proust as "longer and more difficult than the turning inside out of an eyelid, and which consists in the imposition of our own familiar soul on the terrifying soul of our surroundings." He stoops down—cautiously, in the interests of his heart—to unbutton his boots. Suddenly he is filled with a divine familiar presence. Once more he is restored to himself by that being whose tenderness, several years earlier, in a similar moment of distress and fatigue, had brought him a moment's calm, by his grandmother as she had been then, as she had continued to be until that fatal day of her stroke in the Champs-Elysées, after which nothing remained of her but a name, so that her death was of as little consequence to the narrator as the death of a stranger. Now, a year after her burial, thanks to the mysterious action of involuntary memory, he learns that she is dead. At any given moment our total soul, in spite of its rich balance sheet, has only a fictitious value. Its assets are never completely realisable. But he has not merely extracted from this gesture the lost reality of his grandmother: he has recovered the lost reality of himself, the reality of his lost self. As though the figure of Time could be represented by an endless series of parallels, his life is switched over to another line and proceeds, without any solution of continuity, from that remote moment of his past when his grandmother stooped over his distress. And he is as incapable of visualising the incidents that punctuated that long period of intermittence, the incidents of the past few hours, as in that interval he was inexorably bereft of that precious panel in the tapestry of his days representing his grandmother and his love for her. But this resumption of a past life is poisoned by a cruel anachronism: his grandmother is dead. For the first time since her death, since the Champs-Elysées, he has recovered her living and complete, as she was so many times, at Combray and Paris and Balbec. For the first time since her death he knows that she is dead, he knows *who* is dead. He had to recover her alive and tender before he could admit her dead and forever incapable of any tenderness. This contradiction between presence and irremediable obliteration is intolerable. Not merely the memory—the experience— of their mutual predestination is retrospectively abolished by the certainty that it is folly to speak in such cases of predestination, that his grandmother was a chance acquaintance and the few years spent with her an accident, that as he meant nothing to her before their meeting, so he can mean nothing to her after her departure. He cannot understand "this dolorous synthesis of survival and anni- hilation." And he writes:

> I did not know whether this painful and for the moment incomprehensible impression would ever yield up any truth.

> But I knew that if I ever did succeed in extracting some
> truth from the world, it would be from such an impression
> and from none other, an impression at once particular and
> spontaneous, which had neither been formed by my intelli-
> gence nor attenuated by my pusillanimity, but whose dou-
> ble and mysterious furrow had been carved, as by a
> thunderbolt, within me, by the inhuman and supernatural
> blade of Death, or the revelation of Death.

But already will, the will to live, the will not to suffer, Habit, having
recovered from its momentary paralysis, has laid the foundations of its
evil and necessary structure, and the vision of his grandmother begins
to fade and to lose that miraculous relief and clarity that no effort of
deliberate rememoration can impart or restore. It is redeemed for a
moment by the sight of that party wall which, like an instrument, had
transmitted the faltering statement of his distress, and, some days later,
by the drawing of a blind in a railway carriage, when the evocation of
his grandmother is so vivid and painful that he is obliged to abandon
his visit to Mme. Verdurin and leave the train. But before this new
brightness, this old brightness revived and intensified, can be finally
extinguished, the Calvary of pity and remorse must be trod. The
insistent memory of cruelties to one who is dead is a flagellation,
because the dead are only dead insofar as they continue to exist in the
heart of the survivor. And pity for what has been suffered is a more
cruel and precise expression for that suffering than the conscious esti-
mate of the sufferer, who is spared at least one despair—the despair of
the spectator. The narrator recalls an incident that took place during
his first stay at Balbec, in the light of which he had considered his
grandmother as a frivolous and vain old woman. She had insisted on
having her photograph taken by Saint-Loup, so that her beloved
grandchild might have at least that poor record of her latter days, a
fusillade of syncopes (called "symcopes" by the manager of the Grand
Hotel, who now reveals to the narrator this first onslaught of his
grandmother's malady and unwittingly provides, in his absurd mala-
propism, yet another instrument of painful evocation) and strokes
having allowed her to see death clearly at last as a coming event. And
she had been very particular about her pose and the inclination of her
hat, wishing the photograph to be one of a grandmother and not of a
disease. All of which precautions the narrator had translated as the
futilities of coquetry. So, unlike Miranda, he suffers with her whom he

had not seen suffer, as though, for him as for Françoise, whom Giotto's charitable scullion in childbirth and the violent translation of what is fit to live into what is fit to eat leave indifferent, but who cannot restrain her tears when informed that there has been an earthquake in China, pain could only be focussed at a distance.

The Image of Proust

Walter Benjamin

The thirteen volumes of Marcel Proust's *A la recherche du temps perdu* are the result of an unconstruable synthesis in which the absorption of a mystic, the art of a prose writer, the verve of a satirist, the erudition of a scholar, and the self-consciousness of a monomaniac have combined in an autobiographical work. It has rightly been said that all great works of literature found a genre or dissolve one—that they are, in other words, special cases. Among these cases this is one of the most unfathomable. From its structure, which is fiction, autobiography, and commentary in one, to the syntax of endless sentences (the Nile of language, which here overflows and fructifies the regions of truth), everything transcends the norm. The first revealing observation that strikes one is that this great special case of literature at the same time constitutes its greatest achievement of recent decades. The conditions under which it was created were extremely unhealthy: an unusual malady, extraordinary wealth, and an abnormal disposition. This is not a model life in every respect, but everything about it is exemplary. The outstanding literary achievement of our time is assigned a place in the heart of the impossible, at the center—and also at the point of indifference—of all dangers, and it marks this great realization of a "lifework" as the last for a long time. The image of Proust is the highest physiognomic expression which the irresistibly growing discrepancy between literature and life was able to assume. This is the lesson which justifies the attempt to evoke this image.

From *Illuminations*. © 1955 by Suhrkamp Verlag; English translation © 1968 by Harcourt, Brace & World. Schocken Books, 1969.

We know that in his work Proust did not describe a life as it actually was, but a life as it was remembered by the one who had lived it. And yet even this statement is imprecise and far too crude. For the important thing for the remembering author is not what he experienced, but the weaving of his memory, the Penelope work of recollection. Or should one call it, rather, a Penelope work of forgetting? Is not the involuntary recollection, Proust's *mémoire involontaire,* much closer to forgetting than what is usually called memory? And is not this work of spontaneous recollection, in which remembrance is the woof and forgetting the warp, a counterpart to Penelope's work rather than its likeness? For here the day unravels what the night has woven. When we awake each morning, we hold in our hands, usually weakly and loosely, but a few fringes of the tapestry of lived life, as loomed for us by forgetting. However, with our purposeful activity and, even more, our purposive remembering each day unravels the web and the ornaments of forgetting. This is why Proust finally turned his days into nights, devoting all his hours to undisturbed work in his darkened room with artificial illumination, so that none of those intricate arabesques might escape him.

The Latin word *textum* means "web." No one's text is more tightly woven than Marcel Proust's; to him nothing was tight or durable enough. From his publisher Gallimard we know that Proust's proofreading habits were the despair of the typesetters. The galleys always went back covered with marginal notes, but not a single misprint had been corrected; all available space had been used for fresh text. Thus the laws of remembrance were operative even within the confines of the work. For an experienced event is finite—at any rate, confined to one sphere of experience; a remembered event is infinite, because it is only a key to everything that happened before it and after it. There is yet another sense in which memory issues strict weaving regulations. Only the *actus purus* of recollection itself, not the author or the plot, constitutes the unity of the text. One may even say that the intermittence of author and plot is only the reverse of the continuum of memory, the pattern on the back side of the tapestry. This is what Proust meant, and this is how he must be understood, when he said that he would prefer to see his entire work printed in one volume in two columns and without any paragraphs.

What was it that Proust sought so frenetically? What was at the bottom of these infinite efforts? Can we say that all lives, works, and deeds that matter were never anything but the undisturbed unfolding of the most banal, most fleeting, most sentimental, weakest hour in the life of the one to whom they pertain? When Proust in a well-known passage described the hour that was most his own, he did it in such a way that everyone can find it in his own existence. We might almost call it an everyday hour; it comes with the night, a lost twittering of birds, or a breath drawn at the sill of an open window. And there is no telling what encounters would be in store for us if we were less inclined to give in to sleep. Proust did not give in to sleep. And yet—or, rather, precisely for this reason—Jean Cocteau was able to say in a beautiful essay that the intonation of Proust's voice obeyed the laws of night and honey. By submitting to these laws he conquered the hopeless sadness within him (what he once called "*l'imperfection incurable dans l'essence même du présent* [the incurable imperfection in the very essence of the present moment]"), and from the honeycombs of memory he built a house for the swarm of his thoughts. Cocteau recognized what really should have been the major concern of all readers of Proust and yet has served no one as the pivotal point of his reflections or his affection. He recognized Proust's blind, senseless, frenzied quest for happiness. It shone from his eyes; they were not happy, but in them there lay fortune as it lies in gambling or in love. Nor is it hard to say why this paralyzing, explosive will to happiness which pervades Proust's writings is so seldom comprehended by his readers. In many places Proust himself made it easy for them to view this *œuvre*, too, from the time-tested, comfortable perspective of resignation, heroism, asceticism. After all, nothing makes more sense to the model pupils of life than the notion that a great achievement is the fruit of toil, misery, and disappointment. The idea that happiness could have a share in beauty would be too much of a good thing, something that their *ressentiment* would never get over.

There is a dual will to happiness, a dialectics of happiness: a hymnic and an elegiac form. The one is the unheard-of, the unprecedented, the height of bliss; the other, the eternal repetition, the eternal restoration of the original, the first happiness. It is this elegiac idea of happiness—it could also be called Eleatic—which for Proust transforms existence into a preserve of memory. To it he sacrificed in his life friends and companionship, in his works plot, unity of characters, the flow of the narration, the play of the imagination. Max Unold, one of Proust's more discerning readers, fastened on the "boredom" thus created in Proust's writings and likened it to "pointless stories." "Proust managed to make the pointless story interesting. He says: 'Imagine, dear reader, yesterday I was dunking a cookie in my tea when it occurred to me that as a child I spent some time in the country.' For this he uses eighty pages, and it is so fascinating that you think you are no longer the listener but the daydreamer himself." In such stories— "all ordinary dreams turn into pointless stories as soon as one tells them to someone"—Unold has discovered the bridge to the dream. No synthetic interpretation of Proust can disregard it. Enough inconspicuous gates lead into it—Proust's frenetically studying resemblances, his impassioned cult of similarity. The true signs of its hegemony do not become obvious where he suddenly and startlingly uncovers similarities in actions, physiognomies, or speech mannerisms. The similarity of one thing to another which we are used to, which occupies us in a wakeful state, reflects only vaguely the deeper resemblance of the dream world in which everything that happens appears not in identical but in similar guise, opaquely similar one to another. Children know a symbol of this world: the stocking which has the structure of this dream world when, rolled up in the laundry hamper, it is a "bag" and a "present" at the same time. And just as children do not tire of quickly changing the bag and its contents into a third thing—namely, a stocking—Proust could not get his fill of emptying the dummy, his self, at one stroke in order to keep garnering that third thing, the image which satisfied his curiosity—indeed, assuaged his homesickness. He lay on his bed racked with homesickness, homesick for the world distorted in the state of resemblance, a world in which the true surrealist face of existence breaks through. To this world belongs what happens in Proust, and the deliberate and fastidious way in which it appears. It is never isolated, rhetorical, or visionary; carefully heralded and securely supported, it bears a fragile, precious reality: the image. It detaches itself from the structure of Proust's sentences as that summer day at Balbec—old, immemorial, mummified—emerged from the lace curtains under Françoise's hands.

II

We do not always proclaim loudly the most important thing we have to say. Nor do we always privately share it with those closest to us, our intimate friends, those who have been most devotedly ready to receive our confession. If it is true that not only people but also ages have such a chaste—that is, such a devious and frivolous—way of communicating what is most their own to a passing acquaintance, then the nineteenth century did not reveal itself to Zola or Anatole France, but to the young Proust, the insignificant snob, the playboy and socialite who snatched in passing the most astounding confidences from a declining age as from another, bone-weary Swann. It took Proust to make the nineteenth century ripe for memoirs. What before him had been a period devoid of tension now became a field of force in which later writers aroused multifarious currents. Nor is it accidental that the two most significant works of this kind were written by authors who were personally close to Proust as admirers and friends: the memoirs of Princess Clermont-Tonnerre and the autobiographical work of Léon Daudet; the first volumes of both works were published recently. An eminently Proustian inspiration led Léon Daudet, whose political folly is too gross and too obtuse to do much harm to his admirable talent, to turn his life into a city. *Paris vécu,* the projection of a biography onto the city map, in more than one place is touched by the shadows of Proustian characters. And the very title of Princess Clermont-Tonnerre's book, *Au temps des équipages,* would have been unthinkable prior to Proust. This book is the echo which softly answers Proust's ambiguous, loving, challenging call from the Faubourg Saint-Germain. In addition, this melodious performance is shot through with direct and indirect references to Proust in its tenor and its characters, which include him and some of his favorite objects of study from the Ritz. There is no denying, of course, that this puts us in a very aristocratic milieu, and, with figures like Robert de Montesquiou, whom Princess Clermont-Tonnerre depicts masterfully, in a very special one at that. But this is true of Proust as well, and in his writings Montesquiou has a counterpart. All this would not be worth discussing, especially since the question of models would be secondary and unimportant for Germany, if German criticism were not so fond of taking the easy way out. Above all, it could not resist the opportunity to descend to the level of the lending-library crowd. Hack critics were tempted to draw conclusions about the author from the snobbish milieu of his writings, to characterize Proust's works as an internal affair of the French, a literary supplement to the *Almanach de Gotha.* It is obvious that the problems of Proust's characters are those of a satiated society. But there is not one which would be identical with those of the author, which are subversive. To reduce this to a formula, it was to be Proust's aim to design the entire inner structure of society as a physiology of chatter. In the treasury of its prejudices and maxims there is not one that is not annihilated by a dangerous comic element.

Pierre-Quint was the first to draw attention to it. "When humorous works are mentioned," he wrote, "one usually thinks of short, amusing books in illustrated jackets. One forgets about *Don Quixote, Pantagruel,* and *Gil Blas*—fat, ungainly tomes in small print." These comparisons, of course, do not do full justice to the explosive power of Proust's critique of society. His style is comedy, not humor; his laughter does not toss the world up but flings it down—at the risk that it will be smashed to pieces, which will then make him burst into tears. And unity of family and personality, of sexual morality and professional honor, are indeed smashed to bits. The pretensions of the bourgeoisie are shattered by laughter. Their return and reassimilation by the aristocracy is the sociological theme of the work.

Proust did not tire of the training which moving in aristocratic circles required. Assiduously and without much constraint, he conditioned his personality, making it as impenetrable and resourceful, as submissive and difficult, as it had to be for the sake of his mission. Later on this mystification and ceremoniousness became so much part of him that his letters sometimes constitute whole systems of parentheses, and not just in the grammatical sense—letters which despite their infinitely ingenious, flexible composition occasionally call to mind the specimen of a letter writer's handbook: "My dear Madam, I just noticed that I forgot my cane at your house yesterday; please be good enough to give it to the bearer of this letter. P.S. Kindly pardon me for disturbing you; I just found my cane." Proust was most resourceful in creating complications. Once, late at night, he dropped in on Princess Clermont-Tonnerre and made his staying dependent on someone bringing him his medicine from his house. He sent a valet for it, giving him a lengthy description of the neighborhood and of the house. Finally he said: "You cannot miss it. It is the only window on the Boulevard Haussmann in which there still is a light burning!" Everything but the house number! Anyone who has tried to get the address of a brothel in a strange city and has received the most long-winded directions, everything but the name of the street and the house number, will understand what is meant here and what the connection is with Proust's love of ceremony, his admiration of the Duc de Saint-Simon, and, last but not least, his intransigent French spirit. Is it not the quintessence of experience to find out how very difficult it is to learn many things which apparently could be told in very few words? It is simply that such words are part of a language established along lines of caste and class and unintelligible to outsiders. No wonder that the secret language of the salons excited Proust. When he later embarked on his merciless depiction of the *petit clan,* the Courvoisiers, the "esprit d'Oriane," he had through his association with the Bibescos become conversant with the improvisations of a code language to which we too have recently been introduced.

In his years of life in the salons Proust developed not only the vice of flattery to an eminent—one is tempted to say, to a theological—degree, but the vice of curiosity as well. We detect in him the reflection of the laughter which like a flash fire curls the lips of the Foolish Virgins represented on the intrados of many of the cathedrals which Proust loved. It is the smile of curiosity. Was it curiosity that made him such a great parodist? If so, we would know how to evaluate the term "parodist" in this context. Not very highly. For though it does justice to his abysmal malice, it skirts the bitterness, savagery, and grimness of the magnificent pieces which he wrote in the style of Balzac, Flaubert, Sainte-Beuve, Henri de Régnier, the Goncourts, Michelet, Renan, and his favorite Saint-Simon, and which are collected in the volume *Pastiches et mélanges.* The mimicry of a man of curiosity is the brilliant device of this series, as it is also a feature of his entire creativity in which his passion for vegetative life cannot be taken seriously enough. Ortega y Gasset was the first to draw attention to the vegetative existence of Proust's characters, which are planted so firmly in their social habitat, influenced by the position of the sun of aristocratic favor, stirred by the wind that blows from Guermantes or Méséglise, and inextricably intertwined in the thicket of their fate. This is the environment that gave rise to the poet's mimicry. Proust's most accurate, most convincing insights fasten on their objects as insects fasten on leaves, blossoms, branches, betraying nothing of their existence until a leap, a beating of wings, a vault, show the startled observer that some incalculable individual life has imperceptibly crept into an alien world. The true reader of Proust is constantly jarred by small shocks. In the parodies he finds again, in the guise of a play with "styles," what affected him in an altogether different way as this spirit's struggle for survival under the leafy canopy of society. At this point we must say something about the close and fructifying interpenetration of these two vices, curiosity and flattery. There is a revealing passage in the writings of Princess Clermont-Tonnerre. "And finally we cannot suppress the fact that Proust became enraptured with the study of domestic servants—whether it be that an element which he encountered nowhere else intrigued his investigative faculties or that he envied servants their greater opportunities for observing the intimate details of things that aroused his interest. In any case, domestic servants in their various embodiments and types were his passion." In the exotic shadings of a Jupien, a Monsieur Aimé, a Célestine Albalat, their ranks extend from Françoise, a figure with the coarse, angular features of St. Martha that seems to be straight out of a Book of Hours, to those grooms and *chasseurs* who are paid for loafing rather than working. And perhaps the greatest concentration of this connoisseur of ceremonies was reserved for the depiction of these lower ranks. Who can tell how much servant curiosity became part of Proust's flattery, how much servant flattery became mixed with his curiosity, and where this artful copy of the role of the servant on the heights of the social scale had its limits? Proust presented such a copy, and he could not help doing so, for, as he once admitted, "*voir*" and "*désirer imiter*" were one and the same thing to him. This attitude, which was both sovereign and obsequious, has been preserved by Maurice Barrès in the most apposite words that have ever been written about Proust: "*Un poète persan dans une loge de portière* [a Persian poet in a porter's lodge]."

There was something of the detective in Proust's curiosity. The upper ten thousand were to him a clan of criminals, a band of conspirators beyond compare: the Camorra of consumers. It excludes from its world everything that has a part in production, or at least demands that this part be gracefully and bashfully concealed behind the kind of manner that is sported by the polished professionals of consumption. Proust's analysis of snobbery, which is far more important than his apotheosis of art, constitutes the apogee of his criticism of society. For the attitude of the snob is nothing but the consistent, organized, steely view of life from the chemically pure standpoint of the consumer. And because even the remotest as well as the most primitive memory of nature's productive forces was to be banished from this satanic magic world, Proust found a perverted relationship more serviceable than a normal one even in love. But the pure consumer is the pure exploiter—logically and theoretically—and in Proust he is that in the full concreteness of his actual historical existence. He is concrete because he is impenetrable and elusive. Proust describes a class which is everywhere pledged to camouflage its material basis and for this very reason is attached to a feudalism which has no intrinsic economic significance but is all the more serviceable as a mask of the upper middle class. This disillusioned, merciless deglamorizer of the ego, of love, of morals—

for this is how Proust liked to view himself—turns his whole limitless art into a veil for this one most vital mystery of his class: the economic aspect. He did not mean to do it a service. Here speaks Marcel Proust, the hardness of his work, the intransigence of a man who is ahead of his class. What he accomplishes he accomplishes as its master. And much of the greatness of this work will remain inaccessible or undiscovered until this class has revealed its most pronounced features in the final struggle.

III

In the last century there was an inn by the name of "Au Temps Perdu" at Grenoble; I do not know whether it still exists. In Proust, too, we are guests who enter through a door underneath a suspended sign that sways in the breeze, a door behind which eternity and rapture await us. Fernandez rightly distinguished between a *thème de l'éternité* and a *thème du temps* in Proust. But his eternity is by no means a platonic or a utopian one; it is rapturous. Therefore, if "time reveals a new and hitherto unknown kind of eternity to anyone who becomes engrossed in its passing," this certainly does not enable an individual to approach "the higher regions which a Plato or Spinoza reached with one beat of the wings." It is true that in Proust we find rudiments of an enduring idealism, but it would be a mistake to make these the basis of an interpretation, as Benoist-Méchin has done most glaringly. The eternity which Proust opens to view is convoluted time, not boundless time. His true interest is in the passage of time in its most real—that is, space-bound—form, and this passage nowhere holds sway more openly than in remembrance within and aging without. To observe the inter-action of aging and remembering means to penetrate to the heart of Proust's world, to the universe of convolution. It is the world in a state of resemblances, the domain of the *correspondances;* the Romanticists were the first to comprehend them and Baudelaire embraced them most fervently, but Proust was the only one who managed to reveal them in our lived life. This is the work of the *mémoire involontaire*, the rejuvenating force which is a match for the inexorable process of aging. When the past is reflected in the dewy fresh "instant," a painful shock of rejuvenation pulls it together once more as irresistibly as the Guermantes way and Swann's way become intertwined for Proust when, in the thirteenth volume, he roams about the Combray area for the last time and discovers the intertwining of the roads. In a trice the landscape jumps about like a child. *"Ah! que le monde est grand à la clarté des lampes! Aux yeux du souvenir que le monde est petit!* [Oh, how large the world is in the brightness of the lamps. How small the world is in the eyes of recollection.]" Proust has brought off the tremendous feat of letting the whole world age by a lifetime in an instant. But this very concentration in which things that normally just fade and slumber consume themselves in a flash is called rejuvenation. *A la recherche du temps perdu* is the constant attempt to charge an entire lifetime with the utmost awareness. Proust's method is actualization, not reflection. He is filled with the insight that none of us has time to live the true dramas of the life that we are destined for. This is what ages us—this and nothing else. The wrinkles and creases on our faces are the registration of the great passions, vices, insights that called on us; but we, the masters, were not home.

Since the spiritual exercises of Loyola there has hardly been a more radical attempt at self-absorption. Proust's, too, has as its center a loneliness which pulls the world down into its vortex with the force of a maelstrom. And the overloud and inconceivably hollow chatter which comes roaring out of Proust's novels is the sound of society plunging down into the abyss of this loneliness. This is the location of Proust's invectives against friendship. It was a matter of perceiving the silence at the bottom of this crater, whose eyes are the quietest and most absorbing. Something that is manifested irritatingly and capriciously in so many anecdotes is the combination of an unparalleled intensity of conversation with an unsurpassable aloofness from his partner. There has never been anyone else with Proust's ability to show us things; Proust's pointing finger is unequaled. But there is another gesture in amicable togetherness, in conversation: physical contact. To no one is this gesture more alien than to Proust. He cannot touch his reader either; he could not do so for anything in the world. If one wanted to group literature around these poles, dividing it into the directive and the touching kind, the core of the former would be the work of Proust, the core of the latter, the work of Péguy. This is basically what Fernandez has formulated so well: "Depth, or, rather, intensity, is always on his side, never on that of his partner." This is demonstrated brilliantly and with a touch of cynicism in Proust's literary criticism, the most significant document of which is an essay that came into being on the high level of his fame and the low level of his deathbed: "A propos de Baudelaire." The essay is Jesuitic in its acquiescence in his own maladies, immoderate in the garrulousness of a man who is resting, frightening in the indifference of a man marked by death who wants to speak out once more, no matter on what subject. What inspired Proust here in the face of death also shaped him in his intercourse with his contemporaries: so spasmodic and harsh an alternation of sarcasm and tenderness that its recipients threatened to break down in exhaustion.

The provocative, unsteady quality of the man affects even the reader of his works. Suffice it to recall the endless succession of "*soit que . . .*," by means of which an action is shown in an exhaustive, depressing way in the light of the countless motives upon which it may have been based. And yet these paratactic sequences reveal the point at which weakness and genius coincide in Proust: the intellectual renunciation, the tested skepticism with which he approached things. After the self-satisfied inwardness of Romanticism Proust came along, determined, as Jacques Rivière puts it, not to give the least credence to the "*Sirènes intérieures.*" "Proust approaches experience without the slightest metaphysical interest, without the slightest penchant for construction, without the slightest tendency to console." Nothing is truer than that. And thus the basic feature of this work, too, which Proust kept proclaiming as being planned, is anything but the result of construction. But it is as planned as the lines on the palm of our hand or the arrangement of the stamen in a calyx. Completely worn out, Proust, that aged child, fell back on the bosom of nature—not to drink from it, but to dream to its heartbeat. One must picture him in this state of weakness to understand how felicitously Jacques Rivière interpreted the weakness when he wrote: "Marcel Proust died of the same inexperience which permitted him to write his works. He died of ignorance of the world and because he did not know how to change the conditions of his life which had begun to crush him. He died because he did not know how to make a fire or open a window." And, to be sure, of his psychogenic asthma.

The doctors were powerless in the face of this malady; not so the writer, who very systematically placed it in his service. To begin with the most external aspect, he was a perfect stage director of his sickness. For months he connected, with devastating irony, the image of an admirer who had sent him flowers with their odor, which he found unbearable. Depending on the ups and downs of his malady he alarmed his friends, who dreaded and longed for the moment when the writer would suddenly appear in their drawing rooms long after midnight— *brisé de fatigue* and for just five minutes, as he said—only to stay till the gray of dawn, too tired to get out of his chair or interrupt his conversation. Even as a writer of letters he extracted the most singular effects from his malady. "The wheezing of my breath is drowning out the sounds of my pen and of a bath which is being drawn on the floor below." But that is not all, nor is it the fact that his sickness removed him from fashionable living. This asthma became part of his art—if indeed his art did not create it. Proust's syntax rhythmically and step by step reproduces his fear of suffocating. And his ironic, philosophical, didactic reflections invariably are the deep breath with which he shakes off the weight of memories. On a larger scale, however, the threatening, suffocating crisis was death, which he was constantly aware of, most of all while he was writing. This is how death confronted Proust, and long before his malady assumed critical dimensions—not as a hypochondriacal whim, but as a *"réalité nouvelle,"* that new reality whose reflections on things and people are the marks of aging. A physiology of style would take us into the innermost core of this creativeness. No one who knows with what great tenacity memories are preserved by the sense of smell, and smells not at all in the memory, will be able to call Proust's sensitivity to smells accidental. To be sure, most memories that we search for come to us as visual images. Even the free-floating forms of the *mémoire involontaire* are still in large part isolated, though enigmatically present, visual images. For this very reason, anyone who wishes to surrender knowingly to the innermost overtones in this work must place himself in a special stratum—the bottommost—of this involuntary memory, one in which the materials of memory no longer appear singly, as images, but tell us about a whole, amorphously and formlessly, indefinitely and weightily, in the same way as the weight of his net tells a fisherman about his catch. Smell—that is the sense of weight of someone who casts his nets into the sea of the *temps perdu.* And his sentences are the entire muscular activity of the intelligible body; they contain the whole enormous effort to raise this catch.

For the rest, the closeness of the symbiosis between this particular creativity and this particular malady is demonstrated most clearly by the fact that in Proust there never was a breakthrough of that heroic defiance with which other creative people have risen up against their infirmities. And therefore one can say, from another point of view, that so close a complicity with life and the course of the world as Proust's would inevitably have led to ordinary, indolent contentment on any basis but that of such great and constant suffering. As it was, however, this malady was destined to have its place in the great work process assigned to it by a furor devoid of desires or regrets. For the second time there rose a scaffold like Michelangelo's on which the artist, his head thrown back, painted the Creation on the ceiling of the Sistine Chapel: the sickbed on which Marcel Proust consecrates the countless pages which he covered with his handwriting, holding them up in the air, to the creation of his microcosm.

Proust and Evil

Georges Bataille

THE LOVE OF TRUTH AND JUSTICE AND MARCEL PROUST'S SOCIALISM

The passion for truth and justice often gives those who experience it a start. Those who experience it? But surely to desire truth and justice is the same thing as to be a man, to be human. However unequally distributed such a passion may be, it marks the extent to which each man is human—to which human dignity is due to him. Marcel Proust wrote in *Jean Santeuil:*

> It is always with a joyful and positive emotion that we hear those bold statements made by men of science who, for a mere question of professional honour, come to tell the truth—a truth which only interests them because it is true, and which they have to cherish in their art without hesitating to displease those who see it in a very different light and who regard it as part of a mass of considerations which interest them very little.

The style and the content of this passage are very different from *A la recherche du temps perdu*. Yet, in the same book, the style changes, but not the thought:

> What moves us so much in *Phaedo* is that, as we follow Socrates' arguments, we suddenly have the extraordinary

feeling that we are listening to an argument whose purity is unaltered by any personal desire. We feel as if truth were superior to everything, because we realise that the conclusion that Socrates is going to draw is that he must die.

Marcel Proust wrote about the Dreyfus case around 1900. His *dreyfusard* sympathies are known to us all, but after *A la recherche du temps perdu,* written ten years later, he lost his ingenuous aggressiveness. We ourselves have also lost that simplicity. The same passion may occasionally arouse us, but, on the whole, we are too tired, too indifferent. A Dreyfus case in our day would probably cause little stir. . . .

When we read *Jean Santeuil* we are amazed at the importance that politics had for Proust when he was thirty. Many readers will be astonished to see young Marcel boiling with rage because he was unable to applaud Jaurès's words in the Chamber of Deputies. In *Jean Santeuil* Jaurès appears under the name of Couzon. His black hair is curly but there is no room for doubt: he is "the leader of the socialist party in the Chamber . . . the only great orator of our time, the equal of the greatest in antiquity." Proust referred to "the feeling of justice which sometimes seized him like a kind of inspiration." He depicted "the odious imbeciles," the deputies of the majority, "a sarcastic bunch who used their numerical superiority and the strength of their stupidity to attempt to drown the voice of Justice, which was ready to burst into song." Such sentiments are all the more surprising, coming as they do from a man whom one imagines to have been fairly indifferent to politics. The indifference into which he lapsed had several causes. There were, of course, his sexual obsessions. Then there was the fact that the bourgeoisie to which he belonged was threatened by the agitation of the working classes. Yet lucidity also played a part in the exhaustion of his youthful and revolutionary fervour.

Such fervour, we should bear in mind, was based on sentiments completely alien to politics. It was "hostility to his parents which aroused his unbounded enthusiasm for the actions of [Jaurès]." This, admittedly, is Jean Santeuil speaking, but his character is that of Proust. We now know things that we would never have known had it not been for the publication of *Jean Santeuil*. We know that, in his youth, Proust had socialist sympathies, though he did, of course, have certain reservations. "Whenever Jean really thought about it, he was amazed that [Jaurès] allowed his papers to print—indeed, that he himself was prepared to utter—such violent, almost slanderous, even cruel attacks against certain members of the majority." Though it is not the major obstacles in current politics which obstruct the truth, these obstacles had been known for some time. Proust's words might even be banal were they not impregnated with such gaucherie:

> Life, and above all politics, are surely a struggle, and since the wicked carry every weapon, it is the duty of the righteous to carry the same weapons, if only in order to rescue justice. We could almost say . . . that justice perishes because it is inadequately armed. But people will argue that if the great revolutionaries had looked at it too closely justice would never have triumphed.

Proust was tormented by doubt from the start, and his preoccupations lacked consistency: he was no more than bothered by them. Yet, if he could forget them, it was only after he had fathomed their meaning and given his motives. In the fifth part of *Jean Santeuil* Jaurès, who would once "have blushed at the mere idea of shaking a dishonest man by the hand," who "had constituted the very measure of justice for Jean" (the hero of the book), could not, when the time came, "help crying when he thought of everything that he had sacrificed to his duty as party leader."

The plot of the book required Jaurès-Couzon to oppose a slanderous campaign against Jean's father. But, however great the author's affection for him, the politician could not "alienate all those who had fought for him. He could not ruin his life's work and compromise the victory of his ideas in an attempt—a useless attempt because, were he to act alone, it was doomed to failure—to rehabilitate a moderate element who was wrongly suspected." "His passion for honesty, the difficulties he had encountered as he led it to victory, had forced him to identify his conduct with that of the strongest party to which he was obliged to sacrifice his personal preferences in exchange for the help which it gave him." Jean's voice, a voice from the past, from the time when the opposition still had some meaning, concludes with an ingenuousness which may now seem strange:

> You sacrifice the good of all not to a particular friendship, but to a particular interest—to your political situation. Yes, the good of all. Because when they are unjust towards my father, the journalists are not only being unjust. They make their readers unjust. They make them wicked. They make

them want to say that one of their neighbours, whom they thought was good, is wicked . . . I believe that they will triumph one day, and that this triumph will be the triumph of Injustice. As they await the day when the government becomes unjust and injustice will really exist, they make calumny and the love of scandal and cruelty reign in every heart.

Morality in Connection with Transgression of the Moral Law

So ingenuous a tone is surprising in so disingenuous a writer. But can we let ourselves be taken in by what, for a moment, seems to have been his innermost conviction? All we are really left with is the admission of a first instinct. Nobody will be surprised to read these words in the third volume of *Jean Santeuil:* "how often do we write that 'There is only one truly base thing which dishonours the creature which God has created in His image—lying.'? This means that what we really want to avoid is being lied to. It does not mean that we really believe it." Proust then added:

> Jean did not admit (to his mistress) that he had seen the letter through the envelope, and since he could not help telling her that a young man had come to visit her, he said that he had heard it from somebody who had seen her—a lie. But this did not prevent his eyes from filling with tears when he told her that the only truly atrocious thing was a lie.

Carried away by jealousy, the man who had accused Jaurès became a cynic.

Nevertheless this youthful and ingenuous honesty is an interesting phenomenon. In *A la recherche du temps perdu* the evidence of Marcel's cynicism accumulates when jealousy drives him to tortuous manoeuvres. But these very different forms of behaviour, which initially seem to exclude each other, merge. If we had no scruples, if we did not care to observe rigid taboos, we would not be human beings. But we are unable to observe these taboos for ever—if we did not occasionally have the courage to break them, we would find ourselves in a cul-de-sac. It is also true that we would not be human if we had never had, if we had not once had, the heart to be unjust. We ridicule the contradiction between war and the universal taboo which condemns murder, but war, like the taboo, is universal. Murder is always laden with horror, while acts of war are always considered valorous. The same applies to lies and injustice. In certain places taboos have indeed been rigorously observed, but the timid man, who never dares break the law, who turns away, is everywhere despised. The idea of virility always contains the image of the man who, within his limitations, can put himself above the law deliberately, fearlessly and thoughtlessly. Had Jaurès yielded to justice he would not only have injured his supporters: his supporters would have considered him hopelessly incompetent. Virility has a deaf side which commands us never to provide an answer or offer an explanation. We must be loyal, scrupulous and disinterested, but beyond these scruples, this loyalty and this disinterestedness, we must be sovereign.

The necessity of at one point violating the taboo, even if it be sacred, does not invalidate the principle. The man who lied and, as he lied, claimed that "the only truly atrocious thing was a lie" loved truth until he died. Emmanuel Berl has given us a description of the effect Proust's integrity had on him:

> One night, after I had left Proust's house at about three in the morning (it was during the war), I found myself alone in the boulevard Haussman, bewildered and harassed by a conversation which had exhausted both my physical and intellectual resources. I felt that I was at the end of my tether. I was almost as bewildered as I had been when my shelter in Boisle-Prêtre collapsed. I could no longer bear anything, starting with myself. I was exhausted and ashamed of my exhaustion. I thought about this man who hardly ate, who was stifled by asthma and was unable to sleep, but at the same time fought against lies as unhesitatingly as he fought against death. He did not stop before analysis or the difficulty of formulating the results of analysis. He was even prepared to make the additional effort to sort out the cowardly confusion of my own ideas. I was less disgusted by my confusion than by my listlessness in putting up with it.

Such avidity is by no means contrary to the transgression of a point within its own principle. It is too great for the principle to be threatened—even hesitation would be a weakness. At the basis of every virtue is our power to break its hold. Traditional education has neglected this secret resource of morality, and the idea of morality is enfeebled by it. If we place ourselves on the side of virtue moral life appears like a timorous conformism. If we stand on the other side, contempt for insipidity is considered immoral. Traditional education seeks in vain for a surface discipline composed of logical formalism: it turns its back on the spirit of discipline. When Nietzsche denounced traditional morality he thought he would never survive a crime he might have committed. If there is an authentic morality, its existence is always at stake. True hatred of lying acknowledges, after overcoming its disgust, the risk contained in telling a lie. Indifference to risk is due to its apparent lightness. It is the reverse of eroticism which acknowledges the condemnation without which it would be insipid. The concept of intangible laws removes some of its power from a moral truth to which we should adhere, but without tying ourselves down to it. In erotic excess we venerate the rule which we break. A series of rebounding oppositions lies at the basis of an instinct composed alternately of fidelity and revolt, which is the essence of man. Outside this series we are stifled by the logic of laws.

PLEASURE BASED ON THE CRIMINAL SENSE OF EROTICISM

By relating his experience of erotic life, Proust has provided us with an intelligible aspect of this fascinating series of oppositions. One scholar has spotted, in a somewhat arbitrary manner, the symptoms of a pathological state in the association between murder and sacrilege and the absolutely holy image of the mother. "While pleasure held me more and more firmly in its grip," writes the narrator of *A la recherche du temps perdu,* "I felt infinite sadness and desolation aroused in the depths of my heart; I thought I made my mother's soul weep." Sensual pleasure depended on this feeling of horror. At one point in *A la recherche du temps perdu* Marcel's mother disappears, though no mention is made of her death: only his grandmother's death is reported. As if his mother's death meant too much for him, Marcel writes of his grandmother: "Comparing my grandmother's death to that of Albertine, I thought that my life was branded by a double murder."

To the stigma of assassination was added another, still deeper stigma: that of profanation. Let us examine the passage in *Sodome et Gomorrhe* where "the sons, not always resembling their father, fulfil the profanation of their mother in their faces." The author concludes: "Let us abandon at this point a topic which deserves a chapter to itself." Indeed, the key to this particular tragedy is the episode when

Vinteuil's daughter, whose father had died from grief at her behaviour, made love, in her mourning clothes, a few days after the funeral, with a lesbian who spat on the dead man's photograph. Vinteuil's daughter personifies Marcel, and Vinteuil is Marcel's mother. Mademoiselle Vinteuil's invitation to her lover to stay while her father was still alive is a parallel to the narrator's inviting Albertine (in real life the chauffeur Albert Agostinelli) to stay in his apartment. Nothing is said about the mother's reaction to the guest. I imagine that no reader can fail to have noticed that in this the story is imperfect. Vinteuil's death, on the other hand, is recounted in detail. The blank spaces left by Proust are filled in by the passages concerning Vinteuil, which prove so distressing to read if we alter the names.

> For those who, like ourselves, saw [Marcel's mother] avoiding [her] acquaintances, turning away when [she] saw them, aged in a few months, consumed by misery, becoming incapable of any effort which was not aimed directly at [her son's] happiness, spending entire days before [her husband's] tomb, it would be hard not to realise that [she] was dying of misery and to suppose that [she] was unaware of the rumours in circulation. [She] knew about them; [she] may even have confirmed them. There is surely not one person, however virtuous, whom the complexity of circumstances cannot one day oblige to live in familiarity with the vice he condemns most outrightly, without his recognising it fully beneath the disguise of the particular facts which it dons in order to enter into contact with him and make him suffer: bizarre words, inexplicable attitudes, on a certain evening, of a certain person whom he has so many reasons to love. But [a woman] like [Marcel's mother] suffered more than most people when she resigned herself to one of those situations which we mistakenly regard as the exclusive prerogatives of the Bohemian world: they occur every time a vice, nurtured by nature herself in a child, requires the place and security necessary for its indulgence. . . . But the fact that [Marcel's mother] may have known about [her son's] behaviour by no means diminished [her] adoration of [him]. Facts do not penetrate the world of our beliefs; they do not give birth to them, any more than they destroy them.

We can also attribute to Marcel that which is attributed, in *A la recherche du temps perdu,* to Mademoiselle Vinteuil:

> In [Marcel's] heart evil, to start with, at least, was not undiluted. A sadist like [Marcel] is the artist of evil in a way that an entirely evil creature could never be, for evil would never be outside him; it would seem quite natural to him; it would never even be clear to him; and since [he] would have no part in virtue, respect for the dead, or filial affection, [he] would have no sacrilegious pleasure in desecrating them. Sadists of [Marcel's] kind are purely sentimental beings, so naturally virtuous that even sensual pleasure seems bad to them—the privilege of the wicked. And when they allow themselves to yield to it for an instant, they try to enter the wicked man's skin and drag their accomplice into it, so as, in one moment, to have the illusion of having escaped from their scrupulous and tender soul into the inhuman world of pleasure.

Proust also added in *Le Temps retrouvé*: "In the sadist—however good he may be, indeed, the better he is the more it exists—there is a thirst for evil which the wicked, acting for other ends (if they are wicked for some admissable reason), can never satisfy." Just as disgust is the measure of love, thirst for Evil is the measure of Good.

The clarity of this picture is fascinating. What is disturbing in it is the possibility of grasping one aspect without its complementary aspect. Evil seems to be understandable, but only to the extent in which Good is the key to it. If the luminous intensity of Good did not give the night of Evil its blackness, Evil would lose its appeal. This is a difficult point to understand. Something flinches in him who faces up to it. And yet we know that the strongest effects on the senses are caused by contrasts. The movement of sensual life is based on the fear which the male inspires in the female, and on the brutal agony of copulation—it is less a harmony than a violence which may lead to harmony, but through excess. In the first place it is necessary to effect a break—union comes at the end of a tournament at which death is the stake. An agonising aspect of love emerges from its multiple experiences. If love is sometimes pink, pink goes well with black, without which it would be a sign of insipidity. Without black, pink would surely lose the quality which affects the senses. Without misfortune, bound to it as shade is to light, indifference would correspond to happiness. Novels describe suffering, hardly ever satisfaction. The virtue of happiness is ultimately its rarity. Were it easily accessible it would be despised and associated with boredom. The transgression of the rule alone has that irresistible attraction which lasting happiness lacks.

The most powerful scene in *A la recherche du temps perdu* (which puts it on a level with the blackest tragedy) would not have the profound significance we attribute to it if this first aspect were not counterbalanced. If pink has to be contrasted with black in order to suggest desire, would this black be black enough had we never thirsted for purity? had it not tarnished our dream *in spite of ourselves*? Impurity is only known by contrast by those who thought they could not do without its opposite, purity. The absolute desire for impurity, artificially conceived by Sade, led him to that sated state in which every blunted sensation, even the possibility of pleasure, ultimately escaped him. Not even the infinite resource offered him by literature (the imaginary scenes of his novels) could satisfy him. He never knew the particular delight of the moral feeling that gives our sins that criminal flavour without which they seem natural, without which *they are natural*.

Proust was more able than Sade. Eager to have his pleasure, he left vice the odious colour of vice—the condemnation of virtue. But if he was virtuous, it was not in order to obtain pleasure, and if he obtained pleasure it was because he had first wanted to obtain virtue. The wicked only know the material benefits of Evil. If they seek other people's misfortune, this misfortune is ultimately their selfish fortune. We only escape the imbroglio where Evil lies concealed by perceiving the interdependence of opposites. To start with I showed that happiness alone is not desirable in itself and would result in boredom if the experience of misfortune, or of Evil, did not make us long for it. The opposite is also true: had we not, like Proust (and, maybe, even Sade), longed for Good, Evil would provide us with a succession of indifferent sensations.

JUSTICE, TRUTH AND PASSION

What emerges from this is the rectification of the common view which inattentively sees Good in opposition to Evil. Though Good and Evil are complementary, there is no equivalence. We are right to distinguish between behaviour which has a *humane* sense and behaviour which has an odious sense. But the opposition between these forms of behaviour is not that which theoretically opposes Good to Evil.

The poverty of tradition is to rest on that feebleness which determines the care of the future. Care of the future is the exaltation of avarice; it condemns improvidence, which squanders. Provident weakness opposes the principle of enjoying the present moment. Traditional morality complies with avarice: it sees the roots of Evil in the preference for immediate pleasure. Avaricious morality is at the basis of justice and the police. If I like pleasure, I deplore repression. The paradox of justice is that avaricious morality ties it to the narrowness of repression, while generous morality sees it as the primary impulse of him who wants every man to have his due, who runs to the assistance of the victim of injustice. Could justice survive without this generosity? and who could say that it was "ready to burst into song?"

Would truth be what it is if it did not assert itself generously against falsehood? The passion for truth and justice is often far removed from the political masses, for the masses, which are sometimes stimulated by generosity, are sometimes moved by the opposite tendency. In ourselves generosity is always contrasted with avarice, just as passion is contrasted with calculation. We cannot yield blindly to a passion which also involves avarice; but generosity transcends reason and is always passionate. There is something passionate, generous, and sacred in us which exceeds the representations of the mind: it is this excess which makes us human. It would be fruitless to talk of justice and truth in a world of intelligent automats.

It was only because he expected something sacred from it that truth aroused the sort of anger in Marcel Proust which terrified Emmanuel Berl. Berl has left us a description of the scene when Proust threw him out of his house, shouting: "Get out! Get out!" Berl had planned to marry and Proust decided that he was lost to his truth. Was this folly? Perhaps, but would truth confer itself on someone who did not love it to the point of folly? I repeat Berl's words:

> His pale face turned still paler. His eyes sparkled with rage. He got to his feet and went into his dressing room to change. He had to go out. I was aware of his energy. Hitherto I had paid little attention to it. His hair was darker and thicker than mine, his teeth healthier, and his heavy jaw seemed exceptionally mobile. His chest, swollen with asthma no doubt, emphasised the breadth of his shoulders. If we

> were to come to blows, as I thought for a second we might,
> I was not sure of being able to hold my own.

Truth—and justice—require calm, and yet they only belong to the violent.

Though our moments of passion remove us from the coarser requisites of political combat, it is as well to keep in mind that the masses can sometimes be moved by a generous wrath. This is surprising but significant: Proust himself emphasised the irreconcilable element which exists between the police and the generosity of the masses. Proust, who worshipped truth, described the passion for justice which once seized him. He imagined himself, under its impact, "furiously returning the blows which the weaker man was receiving. Similarly, on the day he heard that a thief had been denounced, surrounded and then, after a desperate resistance, garrotted by the police, he had wished that he had been strong enough to murder the policeman."

I was moved by this rebellious instinct, so unexpected in Proust. I see it as the association between anger, stifled by prolonged reflection, and wisdom, without which anger is pointless. If the obscurity of wrath and the lucidity of wisdom do not ultimately coincide, how can we recognise ourselves in this world? But the fragments are to be found on the peak—it is there that we grasp the truth, which is composed of opposites, Good and Evil.

The Worlds of Proust

René Girard

Combray is a closed universe. In it the child lives in the shadow of his parents and the family idols with the same happy intimacy as the medieval village in the shadow of the belfry. Combray's unity is primarily spiritual rather than physical. Combray is the vision shared by all the members of the family. A certain order is superimposed on reality and becomes indistinguishable from it. The first symbol of Combray is the magic lantern whose images take on the shape of the objects on which they are projected and are returned in the same way to us by the wall of the room, the lamp shades, and the doorknobs.

Combray is a closed culture, in the ethnological sense of the word, a *Welt* as the Germans would say, "a little closed world" the novelist calls it. The gulf between Combray and the rest of the world is on the level of perception. Between the perception of Combray and that of the "barbarians" there is a specific difference which it is the essential task of the novelist to reveal. The two bells at the entrance provide us with only a symbol, rather than an illustration of that difference. The bell which "any person of the household . . . put . . . out of action by coming in 'without ringing' " and "the double peal—timid, oval, gilded—of the visitors' bell" evoke two totally incommensurable universes.

At a very superficial level Combray is still capable of making out the difference in perceptions. Combray notices the difference between the two bells; Combray is not unaware that *its* Saturday has a color, a tonality all its own. Lunch is moved up an hour on that day.

> The return of this asymmetrical Saturday was one of those petty occurrences, intra-mural, localised, almost civic, which, in uneventful lives and stable orders of society, create a kind of national unity, and become the favourite theme for conversation, for pleasantries, for anecdotes which can be embroidered as the narrator pleases; it would have provided a nucleus, ready-made, for a legendary cycle, if any of us had had the epic mind.

The members of Combray feel a certain solidarity and brotherliness when they discover something which distinguishes them from the outside world. Françoise, the maid, particularly enjoys this feeling of unity. Nothing causes her more amusement than the little misunderstandings occasioned by the family's forgetting, not that Saturdays are different, but that outsiders are not aware of that fact. The "barbarian" amazed at the change in schedule of which he was not forewarned appears slightly ridiculous. He is not *initiated* into the truth of Combray.

"Patriotic" rites spring up in that intermediate zone where the differences between ourselves and others become perceptible without being completely effaced. The misunderstanding is still half voluntary. On a more profound level it is not voluntary at all, and only the author-narrator can bridge the abyss between the divergent perceptions of a *single* object. Combray is incapable, for example, of understanding that apart from the bourgeois, domestic Swann to whom it is accustomed, there exists another aristocratic and elegant Swann, perceived only by high society.

> And so, no doubt, from the Swann they had built up for their own purposes my family had left out, in their ignorance, a whole crowd of the details of his daily life in the world of fashion, details by means of which other people, when they met him, saw all the Graces enthroned in his face and stopping at the line of his arched nose as at a natural frontier; but they contrived also to put into a face from which its distinction had been evicted, a face vacant and roomy as an untenanted house, to plant in the depths of its unvalued eyes a lingering sense, uncertain but not unpleasing, half-memory and half-oblivion, of idle hours spent together.

The novelist is trying to make us see, touch, and feel what men by definition never see, touch, or feel: two perceptive events which are as imperative as they are contradictory. Between Combray and the outside world there is only an appearance of communication. The misapprehension is total but its results are more comic than tragic. We are provided with another example of comic misunderstanding in the imperceptible thanks which Aunt Céline and Aunt Flora give Swann for a present he sent them. The allusions are so vague and distant that no one notices them, but the two old ladies do not for a moment suspect that they may not have been understood.

What is the origin of this inability to communicate? In the case of the "two Swanns" it would seem that it can all be traced to intellectual causes, to a simple lack of information. Certain of the novelist's expressions seem to confirm this hypothesis. The family's *ignorance* creates the Swann of Combray. The narrator sees in this familiar Swann one of the charming *errors* of his youth.

The error is usually accidental. It disappears as soon as the attention of the person involved is drawn to it, as soon as the means of correcting it are provided. But, in the case of Swann the evidence piles up, the truth about him comes in from all sides without the opinion of the family, and especially that of the great-aunt, being in the least affected. It is learned that Swann frequents the aristocracy; *Le Figaro* mentions paintings in "the collection of Charles Swann." But the great-aunt never swerves in her belief. Finally it is discovered that Swann is the friend of Mme de Villeparisis; far from causing the great-aunt to think more highly of Swann, however, this bit of news has the effect of lowering her opinion of Mme de Villeparisis: "How should she know Swann?" says the great-aunt to the grandmother, "A lady who, you always made out, was related to Marshal MacMahon!" The truth, like a bothersome fly, keeps settling on the great-aunt's nose only to be flicked away.

Thus the Proustian error cannot be reduced to its intellectual causes. We must take care not to judge Proust on the basis of one isolated expression, and especially of the particular meaning to which a particular philosopher might limit that expression. We must go beyond the words to the substance of the novel. The truth about Swann does not penetrate Combray because it contradicts the family's social beliefs and its sense of bourgeois hierarchies. Proust tells us that facts do not penetrate the world where our beliefs reign supreme. They neither gave rise to them nor can they destroy them. Eyes and ears are closed

when the well-being and integrity of the personal universe are involved. His mother observes his father, but not too closely, for she
does not want to understand "the secret of his superiorities." The
aunts Céline and Flora possess to an even higher degree the precious
ability of not perceiving; they stop listening the moment the conversation changes in their presence to something which does not interest
them.

> Their sense of hearing . . . would leave its receptive chan-
> nels unemployed, so effectively that they were actually be-
> coming atrophied. So that if my grandfather wished to
> attract the attention of the two sisters, he would have to
> make use of some such alarm signals as mad doctors adopt
> in dealing with their distracted patients; as by beating several
> times on a glass with the blade of a knife, fixing them at the
> same time with a sharp word and a compelling glance.

These defense mechanisms are obviously the result of mediation.
When the mediator is as distant as in the case of Combray, they cannot
be considered Sartrean "bad faith," but rather what Max Scheler in
Ressentiment calls "organic falsehood." The falsification of experience is
not carried out consciously, as in a simple lie; rather the process begins
in advance of any conscious experience at the point at which representations and feelings about value are first elaborated. The "organic
falsehood" functions every time someone wishes to *see* only that which
serves his "interest" or some other disposition of his instinctive attention, whose object is thus modified even in memory. The man who
deludes himself in this way no longer needs to lie.

Combray shies away from dangerous truths as a healthy organism
refuses to digest something which would harm it. Combray is an eye
which blinks out the particles of dust which might irritate. Everyone at
Combray is therefore his own censor; but this self-censorship, far from
being painful, blends with the peace of Combray, with the happiness
of being a part of Combray. And in its original essence, it is identical
with the pious watchfulness with which Aunt Léonie is surrounded.
Everyone makes an effort to keep from her anything which might
disturb her tranquillity. Marcel earns a reprimand for his lack of
consideration when he tells her that during the course of a walk they
had met "someone they didn't know."

In the child's eyes, Aunt Léonie's room is the spiritual center, the
holy of holies of the family house. The night table crowded with *eau de*

Vichy, medicines, and religious pamphlets is an altar at which the high priestess of Combray officiates with the aid of Françoise.

The aunt seems not to be active but it is she who is responsible for the metamorphosis of the heterogeneous data; she transforms it into "Combray lore." Out of it she makes a rich, tasty, and digestible food. She identifies passers-by and strange dogs; she reduces the unknown to the known. Combray owes all its knowledge and truth to her. Combray, "which a fragment of its medieval ramparts enclosed, here and there, in an outline as scrupulously circular as that of a little town in a primitive painting," is a perfect sphere and Aunt Léonie, immobile in her bed, is the center of the sphere. She does not join in the family activities but it is she who gives them their meaning. It is her daily *routine* which makes the sphere revolve harmoniously. The family crowds around the aunt like houses of the village around the church.

There are striking analogies between the organic structure of Combray and the structure of the fashionable salons. There is the same circular vision, the same internal cohesion sanctioned by a system of ritual gestures and words. The Verdurin salon is not simply a meeting place, it is a way of seeing, feeling, judging. The salon is also a "closed culture." Thus the salon will reject anything which threatens its spirtual unity. It possesses an "eliminative function" similar to that of Combray.

The parallel between Combray and the Verdurin salon can be followed all the more easily since the "foreign body" in both cases is the unfortunate Swann. His love for Odette draws him to the Verdurins. His crossing of social lines, his cosmopolitanism, and his aristocratic relations appear even more subversive at the Verdurins than at Combray. The "eliminative function" is exercised with great violence. The great-aunt is satisfied with a few relatively inoffensive sarcasms in reaction to the general feeling of uneasiness caused by Swann. There is no threat to good-neighborly relations; Swann remains *persona grata*. The situation evolves differently in the Verdurin salon. When the "patroness" realizes that Swann cannot be assimilated, the smiles turn to grimaces of hatred. Absolute excommunication is pronounced, the doors of the salon are closed with a bang. Swann is banished to the outer darkness.

There is something strained and rigid about the spiritual unity of the salon which is not present at Combray. This difference is particularly finely drawn at the level of the religious images expressing that unity. The images used to describe Combray are generally borrowed from the primitive religions, from the Old Testament, and from medieval Christianity. The atmosphere is that of young societies in which epic literature flourishes, faith is naïve and vigorous, and foreigners are always "barbarians" but are never hated.

The imagery of the Verdurin salon is completely different. The dominant themes belong to the Inquisition and the witch-hunts. Its unity seems constantly threatened. The patroness is always standing in the breach ready to repulse the attack of the infidels; she nips schisms in the bud; she keeps constant watch over her friends; she disparages distractions which are found beyond her influence; she demands an absolute loyalty; she roots out any sectarian and heretical spirit which compromises the orthodoxy of her "little clan."

How can we account for the difference between the two different types of the sacred which give unity, the one to the Verdurin salon, the other to Combray? Where are the gods of Combray? Marcel's gods, as we have already seen, are his parents and the great writer Bergotte. They are "distant" gods with whom any metaphysical rivalry is completely out of the question. If we look around the narrator, we find this *external mediation* everywhere. Françoise's gods are the family and especially Aunt Léonie; god for Marcel's mother is his father whom she does not examine too closely in order not to cross the barrier of respect and adoration between him and her; the father's god is the friendly but Olympian M. de Norpois. These gods are always accessible, always ready to answer the call of their faithful, always ready to satisfy reasonable demands, but they are separated from mortals by an insuperable spiritual distance, a distance which prohibits any metaphysical rivalry. In one of the passages of *Jean Santeuil* which present a sketch of Combray can be found a veritable allegory of this collective external mediation. A swan symbolizes the mediator in the almost feudal universe of middle-class childhood. In this closed and protected universe the prevailing impression is one of joy:

> Nor from that general rapture was the swan [excepted], moving slowly on the river bearing, he too, the gleam of light and happiness on his resplendent body . . . never, for a moment, disturbing the happiness about him, but showing by his joyful mien that he, too, felt it though not by a jot changing his slow, majestic progress, as a noble lady may watch with pleasure her servants' happiness, and pass near to them, not despising their gaiety, not disturbing it, but taking in it no part herself save by a show of gracious kindliness and by the presence of a charm shed by her dignity on all around.

Where, then, are the gods of the Verdurin salon to be found? The answer seems easy. In the first place there are the lesser divinities, painters, musicians, and poets, who frequent the salon: more or less ephemeral incarnations of the supreme divinity—ART—whose slightest emanations are enough to throw Mme Verdurin into ecstasies. There is no danger of the official cult going unnoticed. In its name the "Boetians" and the "bores" are banished. Sacrilege is punished more severely than at Combray; the slightest heresy can provoke a scandal. The temptation is to draw the conclusion that faith is more vigorous at the Verdurins than at Combray.

The difference between the two "closed worlds," the more rigid restriction of the salon, would therefore seem to be explained by a strengthening of *external* mediation; at any rate this is the conclusion suggested by appearances. But appearances are deceptive and the novelist rejects this conclusion. Behind the gods of external mediation who no longer have any real power at the Verdurins, there are the true, hidden gods of *internal* mediation, no longer gods of love, but of hate. Swann is expelled in the name of the official gods but in reality we must see here a reprisal against the implacable mediator, against the disdainful Guermantes who close their doors to Mme Verdurin and to whose world Swann suddenly reveals that he belongs. The real gods of the patroness are enthroned in the salon of the Guermantes. But she would rather die than openly or even secretly worship them as they demand. This is why she carries out the rites of her false aesthetic religion with a passion as frenetic as it is mendacious.

From Combray to the Verdurin salon the structure of the "closed little world" does not seem to have changed. The most obvious traits of this structure are merely strengthened and emphasized; the appearances are, if we might be permitted such an expression, more apparent than ever. The salon is a caricature of the organic unity of Combray, just as a mummified face is a caricature of a living face and accentuates its traits. On closer examination it is seen that the elements of the structure, identical in both cases, have a different hierarchy. At Combray the rejection of the barbarians is subordinate to the affirmation of the gods. At the Verdurins it is the reverse. The rites of union are camouflaged rites of separation. They are no longer observed as a means of communion with those who observe similar rites but as a means of distinction from those who do not observe them. Hatred of the omnipotent mediator supersedes love of the faithful. The disproportionate place the manifestations of this hatred hold in the existence of the salon provides the single but irrefutable indication of metaphysical truth: the hated outsiders are the true gods.

The almost identical appearances conceal two very different types of mediation. We are now observing the transition from external to internal mediation not on the level of the individual but on that of the "closed little world." The childhood love of Combray yields to the adult rivalry in hatred, the metaphysical rivalry of snobs and lovers.

Collective internal mediation faithfully reproduces the traits of individual mediation. The happiness of being "among one's friends" is as unreal as the happiness of being oneself. The aggressive unity presented by the Verdurin salon to the outside world is simply a façade; the salon has only contempt for itself. This contempt is revealed in the persecution of the unfortunate Saniette. This character is the faithful of the faithful, the pure soul of the Verdurin salon. He plays, or would play if the salon were really all that it pretends to be, a role somewhat similar to Aunt Léonie's at Combray. But instead of being honored and respected, Saniette is buried under insults; he is the butt of the Verdurins. The salon is unaware that it despises itself in the person of Saniette.

The distance between Combray and the life of the salon is not the distance separating "true" from "false" gods. Nor is it the distance that separates a pious and useful lie from the cold truth. Nor can we agree with Heidegger that the gods have "withdrawn." The gods are nearer than ever. Here the divergence between neoromantic thought and novelistic genius becomes absolutely clear. Neoromantic thinkers loudly denounce the artificial character of a cult confined to accepted values and faded idols in the bourgeois universe. Proud of their perceptiveness, these thinkers never go beyond their first observations. They believe that the source of the sacred has simply dried up. They never stop to wonder what might be hidden behind middle-class *hypocrisy*. Only the novelist looks behind the deceptive mask of the official cult and finds the hidden gods of internal mediation. Proust and Dostoyevski do not define our universe by an absence of the sacred, as do the philosophers, but by the perversion and corruption of the sacred, which gradually poisons the sources of life. As one goes further from Combray the positive unity of love develops into the negative unity of hate, into the false unity which hides duplicity and multiplicity.

That is why only one Combray is necessary while there must be several rival salons. At first there are the Verdurin and Guermantes salons. The salons exist only as functions of each other. Among the collectivities that are simultaneously separated and united by double mediation we find a dialectic of master and slave similar to that which controls the relations of individuals. The Verdurin salon and the Guermantes salon carry on an underground struggle for mastery of the world of fashionable society. For most of the novel the Duchess of Guermantes retains her mastery. Haughty, indifferent, and contemptuous, the hawk-faced Duchess is so dominant that she almost seems the universal mediator of the salons. But like all mastery it proves empty and abstract. Naturally Mme de Guermantes does not see her salon with the eyes of those who long for admittance. If the bourgeois Mme Verdurin, who is supposed to be such an art lover, secretly longs only for aristocracy, the aristocratic Mme de Guermantes dreams only of literary and artistic glories.

For a long time Mme Verdurin is the underdog in the struggle with the Guermantes salon. But she refuses to humble herself and obstinately conceals her desire. Here as elsewhere the "heroic" lie finally wins its reward. The working of internal mediation demands Mme Verdurin's ultimate arrival in the residence of the Prince de Guermantes. As for the Duchess, whose *mastery* has been too blasé, she abuses her power and squanders her prestige. In the end she loses her position in society. The laws of the novel necessitate this double reversal.

Combray is always described as a patriarchal regime; it is impossible to say whether it is authoritarian or liberal since it functions all by itself. The Verdurin salon, on the other hand, is a frenzied dictatorship; the patroness is a totalitarian head of state who rules by a skillful mixture of demagoguery and ferocity. When Proust evokes the loyalist sentiments inspired by Combray, he speaks of *patriotism;* when he turns to the Verdurin salon he speaks of *chauvinism.* The distinction between patriotism and chauvinism is an accurate expression of the subtle yet radical difference between Combray and the salons. Patriotism is the result of external mediation while chauvinism is rooted in internal mediation. Patriotism already contains elements of self-love and therefore self-contempt but it is still a sincere cult of heroes and saints. Its fervor is not dependent upon rivalry with other countries. Chauvinism, on the contrary, is the fruit of such rivalry. It is a negative sentiment based on hatred, that is to say, on the secret adoration of the Other.

Proust's remarks on the First World War, despite their extreme caution, betray a profound disgust. Rose-colored chauvinism is the product of a mediation similar to that of snobbism. The chauvinist hates a powerful, belligerent, and well-disciplined Germany because he himself is dreaming of war, power, and discipline. The revengeful nationalist feeds on Barrès and praises "the earth and the dead" but the earth and the dead are not important to him. He thinks that his roots go deep but he is floating in an abstraction.

At the end of *Remembrance of Things Past* war breaks out. The Verdurin salon becomes the center of the "fight to the bitter end" attitude in society. All the faithful fall in with the patroness's martial step. Brichot writes a belligerent column in a big Paris newspaper. Everyone, even the violinist Morel, wants to "do his duty." Society's chauvinism finds its complement in civic and national chauvinism. The appearance of chauvinism is thus much more than just appearance. Between the microcosm of the salon and the macrocosm of the nation at war there is only a difference of scale. The desire is the same. The metaphors which continually transport us from one dimension to the other draw our attention to this identity of structure.

France is to Germany what the Verdurin salon is to the Guermantes salon. Now Mme Verdurin, the sworn enemy of the "bores," ends by marrying the Prince of Guermantes and removing her arms and baggage into the enemy camp. The rigorous parallelism between social and national chauvinism suggests that we should seek in the order of the macrocosm a parallel to the dramatic reversal in the microcosm, a reversal which can without exaggeration be considered to touch on "treachery." If the novel does not provide this parallel it is simply because it ends too soon. Twenty more years and a second world war are needed to produce the event which would have allowed Proust to round out his metaphor. In 1940 a certain kind of abstract chauvinism embraced the cause of triumphant Germany after years of fulminating against those who timidly suggested a *modus vivendi* with an "hereditary" enemy not yet gone mad and still confined within his own frontiers. Similarly, Mme Verdurin inspires terror in her "little clan" and excommunicates the "faithful" at the slightest sign of weakness toward the "bores," right up to the day when she marries the Prince of Guermantes, closes the doors of her salon to the "faithful," and opens them wide to the worst snobs of the Faubourg Saint-Germain.

Naturally some critics see in the social about-face of Mme Verdurin proof of her "freedom." We are lucky if they do not make use of this so-called freedom to "rehabilitate" Proust in the eyes of current thinkers and to cleanse the novelist of the terrible suspicion of "psychologism." "Look," they say, "Mme Verdurin is capable of abandoning her principles; this character therefore is certainly worthy of participating in an existential novel and Proust, too, is a novelist of *freedom!*"

Obviously these critics are making the same mistake as Jean Prévost when he mistook the political conversion of M. de Rênal for a spontaneous gesture. If Mme Verdurin is "spontaneous" then the enthusiastic "collaborators" are also, since they were fanatical nationalists only a short time before. In reality no one is spontaneous: the laws of double mediation are at work in both cases. The spectacular reprisals against the persecuting divinity always give way to an attempt at "fusion" when circumstances appear favorable. Thus the underground man interrupts his plans of vengeance to write a passionate, raving letter to the officer who insulted him. None of these apparent "conversions" contributes anything new. Here we have no freedom asserting its omnipotence by an authentic break with the past. The convert has not even changed his mediator. We have the illusion of change because we had not recognized a mediation whose only fruits were "envy, jealousy, and impotent hatred." The bitterness of these fruits concealed from us the presence of the god.

The structural identity of the two chauvinisms is again revealed in the expulsion of Baron de Charlus. The affair is a more violent version of Swann's misadventure. Charlus is drawn to the Verdurins by Morel; Swann was attracted by Odette. Swann was the friend of the Duchess of Guermantes; Charlus is her brother-in-law. Thus the Baron is eminently a "bore" and subversive. The "eliminative function" of the salon is exerted against him with particular savagery. The oppositions and contradictions aroused by metaphysical desire are even more obvious and painful than in "Swann in Love" for the mediator has come much nearer.

War has been declared; the account of the themes which accompany the execution of the sentence is colored by the atmosphere of the time. To the traditional terms describing a "bore" is added "German spy." Microcosmic and macrocosmic aspects of "chauvinism" are almost indistinguishable and Mme Verdurin is soon to blend them. She announces to all her visitors that Charlus has been "spying continuously" on her salon for two years.

The sentence reveals very clearly the systematic distortion of the real by metaphysical desire and hatred. This distortion provides the subjective unity of perception. Our immediate thought is that the sentence fits the patroness too well to fit her object too: the Baron de

Charlus. If we have to find the individual essence in an irreducible difference, the sentence cannot reveal the essence of Mme Verdurin without falsifying the essence of the Baron de Charlus. It cannot contain the mutually incompatible essences of both.

Yet this is the miracle it accomplishes. When she declares that Charlus has for two years been a spy in her salon, Mme Verdurin depicts herself, but she also depicts the Baron. Charlus is not, of course, a spy. The patroness exaggerates wildly but she is very well aware of what she is doing; the barb pierces Charlus in the most vulnerable part of his being. Charlus is a terrible defeatist. He is not content to despise Allied propaganda in silence. He launches into subversive suggestions even in the streets. His Germanism chokes him.

Proust analyzes at length Charlus's defeatism. He gives many explanations but the most important of them is homosexuality. Charlus feels a hopeless desire for the handsome soldiers swarming all over Paris. These unattainable soldiers are "exquisite tormentors" for him. They are automatically associated with Evil. The war which divides the universe into two enemy camps provides nourishment for the instinctive dualism of the masochist. The Allied cause being that of the wicked persecutors, Germany must of necessity be associated with the persecuted Good. Charlus confuses his own cause with that of the enemy nation all the more easily that the Germans inspire in him real physical revulsion; he makes no distinction between their ugliness and his own, their military defeats and his own amorous defeats. Charlus is justifying himself when he justifies a crushed Germany.

These feelings are essentially negative. His love for Germany is not nearly as strong as his hatred of the Allies. The frenzied attention he pays to chauvinism is that of the subject to the mediator. Charlus's Weltanschauung is a perfect illustration of the masochistic scheme we described in the preceding chapter. The unity of Charlus's existence becomes even more obvious if we explore his social life, an intermediary zone between his sexual life and his defeatist opinions.

Charlus is a Guermantes. He is the object of an idolatrous cult in the salon of his sister-in-law, the Duchess of Guermantes. He never misses an opportunity, especially in front of his plebeian friends, of proclaiming the superiority of his background, but for him the Faubourg Saint-Germain has none of the fascination it holds for the bourgeois snobs. By definition, metaphysical desire is never aimed at an accessible object. Thus the baron's desires are not drawn by the noble Faubourg but by the lower "riff-raff." This "descending" snobbism explains his passion for the debauched character Morel. The prestige of baseness with which Charlus endows him extends to the whole Verdurin salon. The nobleman can scarcely distinguish this bourgeois hue from the more garish colors which are the normal background of his clandestine pleasures.

Chauvinist, immoral, and bourgeois, the Verdurin salon is a fascinatingly wicked place at the heart of that greater and equally chauvinist, immoral, and bourgeois place, France. The Verdurin salon offers a refuge for the seductive Morel; France at war is full of proud officers. The Baron feels no more "at home" in the Verdurin salon than he does in chauvinist France. But he lives in France and his desire draws him to the Verdurin salon. The Guermantes salon, aristocratic and insipidly virtuous, plays in the Baron's social system a role similar to that of the beloved but distant Germany in his political system. Love, social life, and war are the three circles of this existence which is perfectly unified, or rather perfectly double in its contradiction. All levels correspond and verify the obsessive logic of the Baron.

Thus the counterpart of Mme Verdurin's "chauvinist" obsession is the "antichauvinist" obsession of Charlus. The two obsessions do not isolate the two victims as common sense would expect. They do not close them into two incommensurable worlds; they bring them together in a communion of hatred.

These two existences combine the same elements but organize them inversely. Mme Verdurin claims to be loyal to her salon but her heart is with the Guermantes. Charlus claims to be loyal to the Guermantes but his heart is with the Verdurins. Mme Verdurin praises her "little clan" and scorns the "bores." Charlus praises the Guermantes salon and scorns the "nobodies." We need only reverse the signs to pass from one universe to the other. The disagreement of the two characters is a perfect negative agreement.

This symmetry enables Mme Verdurin to give grotesque but striking expression to the truth about herself and about the Baron in a single sentence. To accuse Charlus of being a spy is Mme Verdurin's secret protest against the scorn of the Guermantes. Common sense cannot see what good it would serve the German High Command to have "detailed reports of the organisation of the little clan." Thus common sense sees through the folly of Mme Verdurin but the more one fixes his attention on her folly the greater the risk that it will fail to see the corresponding folly of Charlus. It is precisely to the extent that she slips into the irrational that Mme Verdurin resembles the Baron.

The madness of one joins the madness of the other in an insane unity, disregarding completely the barriers that common sense would presume to exist between society, life, and the war. Mme Verdurin's chauvinism is aimed at the Guermantes salon and Charlus's defeatism is aimed at the Verdurin salon. Each has only to yield to his madness to understand the other with an acute but incomplete knowledge— acute because passion triumphs over the object-fetishism which paralyzes common sense; incomplete because passion does not perceive the triangle of desire, it fails to recognize the anguish behind the Other's pride and apparent mastery.

In a one-sentence reference of Mme Verdurin to Charlus's "spying" Proust lets us glimpse the complexity of the bonds hatred can weave between two individuals. Mme Verdurin's words reveal both understanding and blindness, a subtle truth and a glaring lie; they are as rich in associations and implications of all kinds as a line of Mallarmé but the novelist is not inventing anything. His genius draws directly on an intersubjective truth which is almost completely unknown to the psychological and philosophical systems of our time.

These words indicate that relationships on the level of the salons and of internal mediation are very different from those established, or rather which cannot be established, at the level of external mediation. As we have seen, Combray is the kingdom of misunderstanding. Since the autonomy is real, relationships with the outside world must of necessity be superficial; no lasting intrigue can be formed. The brief scenes of Combray, like Don Quixote's adventures, are independent of each other. The order in which they succeed each other is almost a matter of indifference for each adventure constitutes a significant totality whose essence is misunderstanding.

Communication would seem to be even more impossible on the level of internal mediation since individuals and salons clash with each other even more violently. As the differences become more acute, any relationship would seem to become impossible in the small worlds which are more and more closed to each other. The aim of all romantic writers is to convince us of precisely this. Romanticism seeks that which is irreducibly ours in that which opposes us most violently to others. It distinguishes two parts in an individual, that which is superficial and permits agreement with others and a more essential part in which agreement is impossible. But this distinction is false and the novelist proves it. The heightening of ontological sickness does not throw the individual out of gear. Mme Verdurin's chauvinism and

Charlus's antichauvinism fit each other perfectly for one is hollow where the other projects. The *differences* displayed by the romantic are the teeth of the gears; they and they alone cause the machine to turn, and they give birth to a *novelistic world* which did not exist before.

Combray was truly autonomous but the salons are not. They are only the less autonomous for their shrill claims to autonomy. At the level of internal mediation, the collectivity, like the individual, ceases to be an absolute reference point. The salons can now be understood only by contrasting them with rival salons, by fitting them into the totality of which each of them is no more than an element.

On the level of external mediation there are only "closed little worlds." The bonds are so loose that there is not as yet any real *novelistic world,* any more than there is a "concert of Europe" before the seventeenth century. That "concert" is a result of rivalry on the national scale. Nations are obsessed with each other. Every day their relationships become closer but they often assume a negative aspect. Just as individual fascination gives birth to individualism, so collective fascination spawns a "collective individualism" which is called nationalism and chauvinism. Individualist and collectivist myths are brothers for they always mask the opposition of the same to the same. The desire to be "among one's friends" just as much as the desire to be oneself hides a desire to be the other.

The "small closed worlds" are neutral particles which have no action on each other. The salons are positive and negative particles which both attract and repel each other, like atomic particles. There are no more monads but semblances of monads which form one vast closed world. The unity of this world, as coherent as that of Combray, is based on an inverse principle. At Combray love still has the upper hand, but hatred generates the world of the salons.

In the hell of *Cities of the Plain* the triumph of hate is absolute. Slaves gravitate around their masters and the masters themselves are slaves. Individuals and collectivities are at once inseparable and completely isolated. Satellites gravitate around planets and planets around stars. This image of the world of the novel as a cosmic system recurs frequently in Proust and brings with it the image of the novelist astronomer who measures the orbits and derives the laws that govern them.

The world of the novel obtains its cohesion from these laws of internal mediation. Only knowledge of these laws makes it possible to answer the question of Vyacheslav Ivanov in his work on Dostoyevski:

"How," the Russian critic asks, "can separation become a principle of union, how can hatred keep the very ones who hate bound together?"

The movement from Combray to the universe of the salons is continuous, with no perceptible transitions. The opposition between *external* and *internal* mediation is not an opposition between Good and Evil, it is not an absolute separation. A closer examination of Combray will reveal, in a nascent state, all the features of the worldly salons.

The great-aunt's ridicule at Swann's expense is an early and faint sketch of the thunderbolts Mme Verdurin and Mme de Guermantes will unleash. The petty persecutions endured by the innocent grandmother prefigure the cruelty of the Verdurins toward Saniette and the frightful coldness of Mme de Guermantes toward her great friend Swann. Marcel's mother refuses, in true bourgeois fashion, to receive Mme Swann. Even the narrator profanes the sacred in the person of Françoise, whom he tries to "demystify." He continually tries to destroy her naïve faith in Aunt Léonie. Aunt Léonie herself abuses her supernatural prestige; she foments sterile rivalries between Françoise and Eulalie; she turns into a cruel tyrant.

The negative element is already present at Combray; thanks to it the closed little world is shut up in itself. It secures the elimination of dangerous truths. This negative element grows gradually larger and ends by devouring everything in the worldly salons. And, as usual, this negative element is rooted in pride and its mediated desire. Pride prevents the great-aunt from perceiving Swann's social position, pride prevents Marcel's mother from receiving Mme Swann. This is but a nascent pride but its essence will not change from one end of the novel to the other. It has scarcely started on its destructive work, but the decisive choice has already been made. The seed of *Cities of the Plain* can already be found in Combray. All that is necessary to move from one universe to the other is to give in to the incline of the slope, to that movement which increases steadily and takes us ever further from the mystic center. This movement is almost imperceptible in Aunt Léonie stretched out in her bed; it becomes more rapid in the child who gazes too hard at the gods of Combray and prepares to succumb to every kind of exoticism.

What is this center which is never reached, which is left further and further behind? Proust gives no direct answer but the symbolism of his work speaks for him and sometimes against him. Combray's center is the church, "epitomising the town, representing it, speaking of it and for it to the horizon." At the center of the church is the steeple of Saint-Hilary, which is for the town what Léonie's room is for the household. The steeple "shaped and crowned and consecrated every occupation, every hour of the day, every point of view in the town." All the gods of Combray are assembled at the foot of this steeple:

> It was always to the steeple that one must return, always it which dominated everything else, summing up the houses with an unexpected pinnacle, raised before me like the Finger of God, Whose Body might have been concealed below among the crowd of human bodies without fear of my confounding It, for that reason, with them.

The steeple is visible everywhere but the church is always empty. The human and earthly gods of external mediation have already become idols; they do not fall in line vertically with the steeple. But they always remain near enough to it so that one glance can encompass Combray and its church. The nearer the mediator comes to the desiring subject the more remote transcendency becomes from that vertical. It is deviated transcendency at work. It drags the narrator and his novelistic universe further and further from the steeple, in a series of concentric circles entitled *Within a Budding Grove, The Guermantes Way, Cities of the Plain, The Captive* and *The Sweet Cheat Gone.* The greater the distance from the mystic center, the more painful, frenzied, and futile becomes the agitation, until we arrive at *The Past Recaptured,* which reverses this movement. This double movement of flight and return is prefigured in the evening pursuits of the crows of Saint-Hilary:

> From the tower windows, it [the steeple] released, it let fall at regular intervals flights of jackdaws which for a little while would wheel and caw, as though the ancient stones which allowed them to sport thus and never seemed to see them, becoming of a sudden uninhabitable and discharging some infinitely disturbing element, had struck them and driven them forth. Then after pattering everywhere the violet velvet of the evening air, abruptly soothed, they would return and be absorbed in the tower, deadly no longer but benignant.

Does Proust's work have a sociological value? It is frequently said that *Remembrance of Things Past* is inferior in this respect to *The Human Comedy* or *The Rougon-Macquart.* We are told that Proust is interested only in the old nobility. His work therefore lacks "breadth and objectivity." Beneath these unfavorable comments we recognize the old realist and positivist conception of the art of the novel. Novelistic genius draws up a detailed inventory of men and things; it should present us with a panorama as complete as possible of economic and social reality.

If this idea were taken seriously, then Proust would be an even more mediocre novelist than they supposed. He is reproached with having "limited his inquiry to the Faubourg Saint-Germain," but that would be giving him credit for more than he attempts. Proust does not embark on any systematic exploration, even in the narrow area which the critics are willing to grant him. He tells us vaguely that the Guermantes are very rich, and that others have been ruined. Where the conscientious novelist would bury us under a heap of records, wills, inventories, accounts, bailiffs' procedures, portfolios of shares and bonds, Proust merely reports a few scraps of conversation over a cup of tea. And he never introduces them for their own sake but simply in relation to something else. There is nothing in all this which warrants the pompous title of *research*. Proust does not even try to suggest, by a definitive tone or an enumeration of unusual objects, that he has "exhausted the documentation."

None of the questions that interest the sociologist seem to attract Proust's attention. We conclude that this novelist is not interested in the problems of society. This indifference, whether it is blamed or praised, is always conceived as a negative element, a kind of mutilation in the service of a particular aesthetic, something similar to the proscription of plebeian words in classical tragedy.

We have learned enough to reject this narrow concept of the art of the novel. The novelist's truth is total. It embraces all aspects of individual and collective existence. Even if the novel neglects some of these aspects it is sure to indicate a perspective. Sociologists can recognize nothing in Proust which reminds them of their own approach because there is a fundamental opposition between the sociology of the novel and the sociology of sociologists. This opposition involves not only the solution and methods but also the data of the problem to be resolved.

In the eyes of the sociologist the Faubourg Saint-Germain is a very tiny but real sector of the social landscape. The frontiers seem to be so clearly fixed that no one questions them. But these frontiers become increasingly blurred the further one reads in Proust's novel. The narrator suffers a terrible letdown when he eventually gains admittance to the Guermantes'! He discovers that the conversation and thought in their salon does not differ from that to which he is accustomed. The essence of the Faubourg seems to vanish. The Guermantes salon loses its individuality and blends into the vague grey of already known milieux.

The Faubourg cannot be defined by tradition since that tradition is no longer understood by so considerable and vulgar a character as the Duke of Guermantes. The Faubourg cannot be defined by heredity since a member of the middle class like Mme Leroi can enjoy a more brilliant social position in it than a Mme de Villeparisis. Since the end of the nineteenth century the Faubourg has not really been a center of political or financial power despite the fact that wealth abounds there and men of influence frequent it in great numbers. Nor is the Faubourg distinguished by a peculiar mentality. It is reactionary in politics, snobbish and superficial in art and literature. There is nothing in all of this to distinguish the milieu of the Guermantes from those of the other idle rich of the early twentieth century.

The sociologist interested in the Faubourg Saint-Germain should not turn to *Remembrance of Things Past*. This novel is not only useless, it can be dangerous. The sociologist thinks he has hold of the object of his research and suddenly he finds it slipping between his fingers. The Faubourg is neither a class, nor a group, nor a milieu; none of the categories currently used by sociologists is applicable to it. Like certain atomic particles, the Faubourg vanishes when scientific instruments are brought to bear on it. This object cannot be isolated. The Faubourg ceased to exist a hundred years ago. And yet it exists because it excites the most violent desires. Where does the Faubourg begin, and where does it end? We do not know. But the snob knows; he never hesitates. It is as if the snob possessed a sixth sense which determined the exact social standing of a salon.

The Faubourg exists for the snob and does not exist for the nonsnob. We should say, rather, that it would not exist for the nonsnob were it not that the latter agrees to accept the snob's testimony in order to settle the question once and for all. Obviously the Faubourg exists only for the snob.

Proust is accused of confining himself to too narrow a milieu but no one recognizes and denounces that narrowness better than Proust. Proust shows us the insignificance of "high society" not only from the intellectual and human angle but also from the *social* point of view:

"The members of the fashionable set delude themselves as to the social importance of their names." Proust pushes the demystification of the Faubourg Saint-Germain much further than his democratic critics. The latter, in fact, believe in the objective existence of the magic object. Proust constantly repeats that the object does not exist. "Society is the kingdom of nothingness." We must take this affirmation literally. The novelist constantly emphasizes the contrast between the objective nothingness of the Faubourg and the enormous reality it acquires in the eyes of the snob.

The novelist is interested neither in the petty reality of the object nor in that same object transfigured by desire; he is interested in the process of transfiguration. This has always been the fundamental concern of the great novelists. Cervantes is not interested in either the barber's basin or Mambrino's helmet. What fascinates him is that Don Quixote can confuse a simple barber's basin with Mambrino's helmet. What fascinates Proust is that the snob can mistake the Faubourg Saint-German for that fabled kingdom everyone dreams of entering.

The sociologist and the naturalistic novelist want only *one* truth. They impose this truth on all perceiving subjects. What they call *object* is an insipid compromise between the incompatible perceptions of desire and nondesire. This object's credibility comes from its intermediate position, which weakens all the contradictions. Instead of taking the edge off these contradictions the great novelist sharpens them as much as possible. He underscores the metamorphoses brought about by desire. The naturalistic writer does not perceive this metamorphosis because he is incapable of criticizing his own desire. The novelist who reveals triangular desire cannot be a snob but he must have been one. He must have known desire but must now be beyond it.

The Faubourg is an enchanted helmet to the snob and a barber's basin to the nonsnob. Every day we are told that the world is controlled by "concrete" desires: wealth, well-being, power, oil, etc. The novelist asks an apparently harmless question: "What is snobbism?"

In his probe of snobbism the novelist is asking himself in his own way just what might be the hidden springs that make the social mechanism tick. But the scientists shrug their shoulders. The question is too frivolous for them. If they are urged to give an answer they become evasive. They will suggest that the novelist is interested in snobbism for the wrong reasons. He himself is a snob. Let us say rather he was one. That is true; but the question remains. What is snobbism?

The snob seeks no concrete advantage; his pleasures and sufferings are purely *metaphysical*. Neither the realist, the idealist, nor the Marxist can answer the novelist's question. Snobbism is the grain of dust that finds its way into the gears of "science" and throws it out of kilter.

The snob desires nothingness. When the concrete differences among men disappear or recede into the background, in any sector whatever of society, abstract rivalry makes its appearance, but for a long time it is confused with the earlier conflicts whose shape it assumes. The snob's abstract anguish should not be confused with class oppression. Snobbism does not belong to the hierarchies of the past as is generally thought, but to the present and still more to the democratic future. The Faubourg Saint-Germain in Proust's time is in the vanguard of an evolution that changes more or less rapidly all the layers of society. The novelist turns to the snobs because their desire is closer to being completely void of content than ordinary desires. Snobbism is the caricature of these desires. Like every caricature, snobbism exaggerates a feature and makes us see what we would never have noticed in the original.

The Faubourg Saint-Germain is a pseudo-object and thus plays a privileged role in novelistic revelation. This role can be compared to that of radium in modern physics. Radium occupies a position in nature as limited as the Faubourg Saint-Germain in French society. But this extremely rare compound possesses exceptional properties which contradict certain principles of the old physics and gradually overthrow all the perspectives of an earlier "science." Similarly, snobbism gives the lie to certain principles of standard sociology; it shows us motives for action never suspected by scientific thought.

The genius of Proust's novel derives from snobbism transcended. His snobbism takes the author to the most abstract place in an abstract society, toward the most outrageously empty pseudo-object—in other words, to the place most suited to novelistic revelation. In retrospect, snobbism must be identified with the first steps of genius; an infallible judgment is already at work, as well as an irresistible impetus. The snob must have been excited by a great hope and have suffered tremendous letdowns, so that the gap between the object of desire and the object of nondesire imposes itself on his consciousness, and that his consciousness may triumph over the barriers erected each time by a new desire.

After serving the author, the caricatural force of snobbism should now serve the reader. In reading we relive the spiritual experience whose form is that of the novel itself. After conquering his truth, the novelist can descend from the Faubourg Saint-Germain to the less rarefied regions of social existence, like the physicist who extends to "ordinary" compounds the facts he has learned from that "extraordinary" compound, radium. In most circles of middle- and even lower-class existence Proust discovers the same triangular structure of desire, the sterile opposition of contraries, hatred of the hidden god, the excommunications and destructive taboos of internal mediation.

This progressive broadening of novelistic truth entails the extension of the term snobbism to the most diverse professions and environments. In *Remembrance of Things Past,* we find a snobbism of professors, doctors, lawyers, and even servants. Proust's uses of the word snobbism define an "abstract" sociology, universal in its application, but whose principles are most active among the very rich and idle.

Thus Proust is far from indifferent to social reality. In a sense this is all he talks of, for to the novelist of triangular desire interior life is already social and social life is always the reflection of individual desire. But Proust stands in radical opposition to the old positivism of Auguste Comte. He is equally opposed to Marxism. Marx's *alienation* is analogous to metaphysical desire. But alienation has little correspondence with anything but external mediation and the upper stages of internal mediation. The Marxist analyses of bourgeois society are more penetrating than most but they are vitiated at the outset by yet another illusion. The Marxist thinks he can do away with all alienation by destroying bourgeois society. He makes no allowance for the extreme forms of metaphysical desire, those described by Proust and Dostoyevski. The Marxist is taken in by the object; his materialism is only a relative progress beyond middle-class idealism.

Proust's work describes new forms of alienation that succeed the old forms when "needs" have been satisfied and when concrete differences no longer control relationships among men. We have seen how snobbism raises abstract barriers between individuals who enjoy the same income, who belong to the same class and to the same tradition. Some of the intuitions of American sociology help us appreciate the fertility of Proust's point of view. Thorstein Veblen's idea of "conspicuous consumption" is already triangular. It deals a fatal blow to materialist theories. The value of the article consumed is based solely on how it is regarded by the other. Only another's desire can produce desire. More recently, David Riesman and Vance Packard have shown that even the vast American middle class, which is as free from want and even more uniform than the circles described by Proust, is also divided into abstract compartments. It produces more and more taboos and excommunications among absolutely similar but opposed units. Insignificant distinctions appear immense and produce incalculable effects. The individual's existence is still dominated by the other but this other is no longer a class oppressor as in Marxist alienation; he is the neighbor on the other side of the fence, the school friend, the professional rival. The other becomes more and more fascinating the nearer he is to the self.

The Marxists explain that these are "residual" phenomena connected with the bourgeois structure of society. Their reasoning would be more convincing if analogous phenomena were not observed in Soviet society. Bourgeois sociologists are only shuffling the cards when they claim, observing these phenomena, that "classes are forming again in the U.S.S.R." Classes are not forming again: new alienations are appearing where the old ones have disappeared.

Even in their boldest intuitions the sociologists do not succeed in completely throwing off the tyranny of the object. None of them has gone as far as novelistic reflection. They tend to confuse the old class distinctions, distinctions imposed externally, with the inner distinctions created by metaphysical desire. It is easy to make this confusion since the transition from one alienation to another covers a long period during which double mediation is proceeding underground without ever coming to the surface. The sociologists never get as far as the laws of metaphysical desire because they do not realize that even material values are finally swallowed up by double mediation. The snob desires nothing concrete. The novelist observes this and traces the symmetrical and empty oppositions of snobbism on all levels of individual and collective life. He shows us how the abstract triumphs in private, professional, national, and even international life. He shows that the First World War, far from being the last of the national conflicts, is the first of the great abstract conflicts of the twentieth century. In short, Proust takes up the history of metaphysical desire at the very point where Stendhal left it. He shows us double mediation crossing national frontiers and acquiring the planetary dimensions which we find that it has today.

After describing social rivalries in terms of military operations, Proust describes military operations in terms of social rivalries. What we considered a moment ago as an image now becomes an object and the object becomes an image. As in contemporary poetry, the two terms of the image are interchangeable. The same desire triumphs in both microcosm and macrocosm. The structure is the same, only the pretext changes. Proust's metaphors deflect our attention from the object and direct it to the mediator; they help us turn from linear desire to triangular desire.

Charlus and Mme Verdurin confuse social life with the First World War; the novelist goes beyond this madness as it in turn had outgrown "common sense." He no longer confuses the two areas, he methodically assimilates them to one another. The novelist for this reason runs the risk of appearing superficial in the eyes of *specialists*. He is accused of explaining big events by "little causes." Historians want history to be taken seriously and they will never forgive Saint-Simon for having interpreted some of Louis XIV's wars in terms of court rivalries. They forget that nothing which concerned Louis XIV's favor could be considered unimportant during his reign.

The distance between pure and simple futility and cataclysmic futility is imperceptible. Saint-Simon is aware of this and so are the novelists. There are, in any case, no "causes" great or small, there is only the infinitely active void of metaphysical desire. The First World War, like the war of the salons, is the fruit of this desire. To be convinced of this, we have only to consider the antagonists. We see the same indignation, the same theatrical gestures, on both sides. The speeches are all the same: to make them admirable or atrocious, depending on the listener, all that is necessary is to reverse the proper names. Germans and French slavishly copy each other. A comparison of certain texts gives Charlus an opportunity for some very bitter laughter.

Some years ago we could still smile at this universal snobbism. A prisoner of his own obsession with society, the novelist seemed to us far removed from contemporary horrors and anguish. But Proust should be reread in the light of recent historical development. Everywhere there are symmetrical *blocs* opposing each other. Gog and Magog imitate and hate each other passionately. Ideology is merely a pretext for ferocious oppositions which are secretly in agreement. The *Internationale* of nationalism and the nationalism of the *Internationale* blend and intersect in inextricable confusion.

In his book *1984*, the English novelist George Orwell portrays directly certain aspects of this historical structure. Orwell clearly understands that the totalitarian structure is always *double*. But he does not show the connection between individual desire and the collective structure. We sometimes get the impression from his books that the "system" has been imposed from the outside on the innocent masses. De Rougemont in *Love in the Western World* goes still further; he is even closer to novelistic insight when he traces the source of collective wills to power and totalitarian structures to that individual pride which originally gave birth to the mystics of passion. "Unmistakably, when rival wills to power confront one another—and there were already *several* Totalitarian States!—they are bound to clash passionately. Each becomes for some other an *obstruction*. The real, tacit, and inevitable aim of the totalitarian elevation was therefore war, and war means *death*."

We are told that Proust has neglected the most important aspects of modern social life, that he does no more than describe a relic of former times, a survival destined to disappear, and which at best is only slightly picturesque. In a way this is true. Proust's little world is rapidly receding from our life. But the great world in which we are beginning to live grows more like it every day. The setting is different, the scale is different, but the structure is the same.

A quarter of a century of this ambiguous historical evolution has made a relatively obscure and difficult work crystal clear. Critics have noticed the growing clarity of this masterpiece and they see in it the result of its own radiance. The novel itself is supposed to be training its own readers and shedding more and more light on the understanding of itself. This optimistic point of view is linked to the romantic idea of the artist as a creator of new values, another Prometheus refining the celestial fire in order to give it to a grateful human race. This theory certainly cannot be applied to the novel. The novel does not contribute new values; with great effort, it reconquers the values of previous novels.

Remembrance of Things Past no longer seems obscure but it is not necessarily better *understood*. The spiritual influence of great novels is weak, as we know, and it is very seldom exerted in the direction anticipated by the author. The reader projects into the work the same meanings he already projects into the world. With the passing of time this projection becomes easier since the work is "ahead" of society, which gradually catches up with it. The secret of this advance is in no way mysterious. In the first place, it is the novelist who feels desire the most intensely. His desire leads him into the most abstract regions and to the most meaningless objects. Thus his desire almost automatically leads him to the summit of the social edifice. As we have already remarked in connection with Flaubert, this is where the ontological sickness is most acute. The symptoms observed by the novelist will gradually spread to the lower layers of that society. The metaphysical situations portrayed in the novel will become familiar to a great number of readers; the oppositions in the novel will find their exact replicas in day-to-day existence.

The novelist who reveals the desire of the social elite is almost always *prophetic*. He is describing intersubjective structures that will gradually become banal. What is true of Proust is also true of other novelists. Almost all the great novelists yield to the temptation of an aristocratic background. In all of Stendhal's novels there is a double movement from the provinces to the capital and from middle-class life to fashionable life. Don Quixote's adventures gradually lead him toward the aristocracy. Stavrogin, the universal mediator of *The Possessed*, is an aristocrat. *The Idiot, The Possessed, The Raw Youth,* and *The Brothers Karamazov* are "aristocratic" novels. Dostoyevski often explains the role of the Russian aristocracy in his novels. Its degeneracy and moral corruption act as a magnifying glass on Russian life, excluding the life of the peasant. If allowance is made for the differences of language and ethical outlook, that is precisely the role played by the aristocracy in the novels of Cervantes, Stendhal, and Proust.

The great novels end in the sterile abstraction of high society because the whole society gradually tends toward that abstraction. Such diverse minds as Paul Valéry and Jean-Paul Sartre have criticized Proust for the frivolity of his book. Everyone says that he does not understand France, that he confuses it with the Faubourg Saint-Germain. We must agree with the critics, but in this brilliant confusion lies one of the great secrets of Proust's creation. Those who portray the social elite are either very superficial or very profound depending on whether they reflect metaphysical desire or whether on the contrary they succeed in revealing it.

The Architecture of Time: Dialectics and Structure

Richard Macksey

As each successive volume of *A la recherche du temps perdu* issued from the cork-lined cell on the boulevard Haussmann, Marcel Proust anxiously wrote to friends and critics to insist once more on the irreducible unity and symmetry of his life work. As the digressions, characters, and reversals multiplied, from the prismatic variety of the world presented there, readers began to select aspects and to make Prousts in their own image: the author as psychologist, memorialist, aesthetician, comedian, martyr of art. And yet the novelist constantly returned in his correspondence to his concern for construction. At times he would analogize his task to that of a composer resolving opposing themes or leitmotivs into a musical structure; more often he would turn to the metaphoric role of architect. It was the master builder alone who could guarantee that the content would be, in fact, embodied in the shape, that the work of years would preserve the coherence of its original plan. Thus, as early as February 1914, Proust wrote in his first letter to Jacques Rivière with an enthusiasm born of anxiety: "At last I have found a reader who has hit upon [*qui devine*] the fact that my book is a dogmatic work and a construction! . . . In this first volume you have seen the pleasure afforded me by the *madeleine* dipped in tea: I say that I cease to feel mortal etc., and that I do not understand why. I will not explain until the end of the third [i.e., last] volume. The whole is so *constructed*." To Benjamin Crémieux, who was later to defend him as

From *Proust: A Collection of Critical Essays,* edited by René Girard. © 1962 by Prentice-Hall, Inc.

the master of the "composition en rosace," the ordering of episodic losenges into an internally related circle like the great rose windows of the French cathedrals, Proust wrote: "Thank you for comparing my book to a city. . . . People fail only too often to realize that my books form a construction, but drawn to a compass so vast that the structure—a rigorous structure to which I have subordinated everything—takes rather a long time to discern. There will be no denying it when the last page of *Le Temps retrouvé* (written before the rest of the book) closes precisely on the first page of *Swann*." The image of an architectural circle in its simplicity and expansiveness thus encloses the entire work, like the medieval wall which encloses Combray and gives it form.

André Maurois proposes another rich architectural image, that of the gothic arch itself, after he quotes this unpublished letter from Proust to Jean Gaigneron [in *A la recherche de Marcel Proust* (Paris, 1949), p. 175]:

> And when you speak to me of cathedrals I cannot fail to be moved by the intuition which lets you guess [*deviner*] what I have never told anyone and am writing here for the first time; that is that I had wanted to give to each part of my book the title: *Porch, Stained Glass of the Apse*, etc., to answer in advance the stupid criticism which claims that I lack construction in books whose only merit, as I shall show you, is in the adherence of the smallest parts.

Through the design of the builder the opposed piers of the gothic arch were enlisted so as to sustain the whole great mass of the towering edifice. And just as in the medieval cathedral moral directions were embodied in space, so the extremes and the unity of Proust's entire work are suggested in his system of structural oppositions, the piers of his building.

For Proust originality was a quality of "vision," a way of seeing the world whole and unique; he saw his own task as that of enclosing his world in a new structure which, like the parish church of Saint-Hilaire, would include in its unity the "four dimensions of space—the name of the fourth being Time." Although the vocabulary of Proust's extended architectural metaphors frequently recalls his apprenticeship to John Ruskin, two insistent points in such comparisons are peculiarly characteristic of the novelist's own vision: the possibility of creating a dialectic between inside and outside, a living space within which the artist can translate the world; and the possibility, usually represented by the gothic arch or rose window, of bringing into immanent contact two apparently opposed views or ways of life.

The world outside, beyond the walls of the family or of Combray, is always the object of the Proustian character in his moment of dispersion; the mechanism by which he reaches out in a vain attempt to appropriate the shifting surfaces out there for his own may be called love or *snobisme* or even chauvinism, but the trajectory is always the same, a flight from the inside, from the center of the self. Although the Proustian world (the author's vocabulary to the contrary) in no way partakes of the Plotinian world of procession, absolute intelligibility, and eternal essences, yet the novelist's model of the soul, with its dialectic of inside and outside, does resemble the Neoplatonic sphere on whose outer surface is displayed the cinematic film of the flux of the senses and on whose inner surface is reflected the light from the center, which is Being itself. The first movement in each case is outward toward the flux, the second a turning back on the center. The negative half of Proust's dialectic, the progressive erosion of appearances by change, has led some critics to recognize the Plotinian attempt to abolish everything in reality which is impervious to spiritual penetration. But for Proust the experience of change and the succession of affective states which it brings is absolutely essential to the later, positive phase of the dialectic—the remembering and reconstituting of these experiences. Plotinus, on the other hand, dismisses memory (in the worldly and non-Platonic sense): "The more the Soul strives after the intelligible, the more it forgets. . . . In this sense, therefore, we may say that the good soul is forgetful."

Again, the image of a space within the structure of consciousness suggests the place where Mallarmé's "rose absent from every bouquet" blooms eternally. The quest for an "interior space" of presence and stability is certainly a familiar aspect of the Symbolist program. Yet the element of Proust's revision which must be emphasized here is again the crucial importance, the necessity, of the *outside* in creating a consciousness through its very opposition. The doors of Proust's edifice of consciousness may be sealed against others, but the fantastic windows, like those of the chapel of Gilbert le Mauvais, do admit the very light whereby newly refracted, altered images are composed within.

Existence for Proust is thus defined in terms of an antinomy: a going out toward primitive experience, hopelessly fragmented into sensational instants, and a return toward the interior of oneself to relate these experiences, these instants, to the past: expansion and concentration. There is no existence without content, then, but the Proustian man (like his counterparts described by Kierkegaard and Sartre) crouches within the edifice of his consciousness, removed from the Other. He demands this distance between as a requisite of his knowing. In the same way he is, in Augustine's "specious present," at some temporal remove from his own existence; he rather seeks to constitute himself in the very consciousness that he *has existed*. Just as Proust argues that all creation is re-creation, so all cognition is recognition. The precarious present moment is sustained by the presence of the past, "the stalk of recollection" of which he speaks at length. This vital activity of the consciousness can only take place with epistemic and temporal distance; the only possible portrait of the artist is as a young man.

While the image of an historical structure like the cathedral illustrates Proust's dialectic of inside-outside with a temporal dimension, the second implication of Proust's architectural imagery is figured by the arch. This image suggests Proust's need to organize his experience in terms of paired opposites and, where possible, to find some unsuspected similarity as keystone to unite them. This habit of mind is at the very heart of his almost sacerdotal attention to metaphor, to synaesthesia, to puns, to stylistic devices such as syllepsis and oxymoron—all pivots on which to engage opposition. These counterstressed elements of style can be considered monads which reflect the construction of the fictional universe, for the entire work unfolds in terms of oppositions: of point of view, of plot development, and of character. Proust is an author of strenuous dualism. Out of opposites, however, is generated the dynamism toward a dialectic. With Anaximander of Miletus, Proust comprehends life as the paired opposition of basic rhythms: Day and Night, Presence and Absence, Time and Intemporality; with Heraclitus of Ephesus he seeks the possible unity of this dualism in change: "way up, down; one and the same." Plato's captious Elean Stranger of the *Sophist* suggests that Heraclitus's cosmology, along with the system of counterstresses developed a generation later, was the first attempt to reconcile Ephesian Opposition with the Eleatic first principle, the One. Hegel dryly glosses the text by remarking that this event was the birth of the dialectics. The attempt to exhaust reality through systems of opposition was, of course, hardly abandoned with the pre-Socratic cosmologies. In fact, Heidegger organizes his *Einführung in der Metaphysik* around four great oppositions which serve to delimit Being: the opposed pairs of Being and Becoming, Being and Appearance, Being and

Thought, and Being and Value. In some sense each of these fundamental sets is posed in Proust's novel.

Now to suggest through the image of the arch or circle that extremities can be reconciled in Proust's world in some dialectical manner immediately invokes the name of Hegel. This philosopher's discovery of his own method through a study of the Kantian categories suggests, at least by analogy, the Proustian "general experience." Thus, whereas the third category, singularity, is for Hegel a synthesis of the preceding two, generality and particularity, Proust seems to discover in the experience of the *extase* a subjective generality mediating between two particular experiences. And yet the word to emphasize in Proust's dialectics is *experience*. Like Kierkegaard and P. J. Proudhon, he is committed to an *affective* and not a rational dialectics; nor does the synthesis destroy the original opposition; Proust is closer to Proudhon's active equilibrium, his "armed union." It is the very isolation of the individual and the Humean discontinuity of time which saves the Proustian man from leaking away dialectically into the Hegelian Absolute. His is not the richly communicable existence of Hegel and Bosanquet, almost nullifying the individual personality in the solemn procession to the whole, the Idea. Heidegger is much closer to Proust's view of things when he sees the phenomenology of the spirit as the mirror image of the true itinerarium of the historical destiny; *Dasein* does not create the things-that-are but discovers them and is in some way dependent on them in the foundation of its horizon. Like Kierkegaard or Nietzsche, Proust develops a pathetic (not an intellectual) dialectics, grounded in the moment: from perceptive immediacy to ecstatic immediacy. The Absolute is conceived more as intensity (of suffering or joy) than as totality: more as immediacy than as mediation.

"JE" EST UN AUTRE

Any investigation of the systems of opposition which are the arches of Proust's construction might well begin with the fictional authority itself. The point of view from which the action is seen is curiously divided between the Marcel of past time who acts and grows old through the course of the narrative, and the Marcel who recollects him from the distant vantage and is at last joined by him to pass, with the final footfall, into time regained. The situation is not unlike that of "Rousseau juge de Jean-Jacques." The division in the narrator underscores the double technique—dramatic and discursive—and the double demonstration—the illusory character of external appearances, minds, and values against the reality and continuity of the self. Thus the action can be likened to an odyssey or pilgrimage where the traveler in time has forgotten the location of the homeland or the significance of the shrine.

The resources available to the narrator in his search are again paired: the voluntary and the involuntary imagination springing from radically different experiences; two kinds of "intelligence," one analytic, rational, dedicated to reducing appearances and behavior to general, axiomatic laws, the other synthetic and intuitive, devoted to the promptings of the involuntary memory or the pure mimetic imagination.

Further, the divided narrator is torn between two conflicting vocations: one, the centrifugal pursuit of the worldly *ignis fatuus*, whether in the guise of a loved object or a social conquest; the other, the centripetal quest for the self and its coherence, which is for Proust the way of art. Before the narrator reaches integration in the last pages, he will pass through the lowest point in his spiritual trajectory when both callings seem to fail him, when disillusionment conspires with acedia.

The Anti-Hero

Through an almost miraculous intervention the narrator does find his course and calling. Yet Proust has installed in his novel a tragic *doppelgänger* who prefigures and parallels the narrator, but who misses the vocation to which he, too, is called. This "anti-hero" has two faces; he is both a spiritual ancestor of Marcel and a glittering contemporary. The technique of displaying successive aspects of essentially the same personality recalls Proust's delight in the Balzacian *retour des personnages:* the successive reincarnations of Vautrin. Paradoxically, in a book where the fiction of stable and coherent characters is constantly being exploded by dramatic reversals and impossible contradictions, the two faces of Marcel's counterpart have in their way a greater consistency than most of the "single" characters. Like the medieval symbol which could be read *in bono* or *in malo*, the novel can be seen as the story of the narrator's salvation through art or the anti-hero's damnation through love. This composite counterpart to Marcel is Charles Swann whose story precedes his, and Palamède de Charlus whose career parallels the narrator's own.

The deflection in time and dramatic focus to the episode of "Un

Amour de Swann" has led some readers to argue that the second panel of the first volume is Proust's virtuoso piece, a novel within a novel, and basically irreconcilable with the theme and technique of the grand plan. And yet on this history of Swann Proust rested one pier of the arch which was to be his double investigation of the artist's vocation. Like *King Lear* the entire work is a double plot, a dramatization of two ways of meeting the world (in one case seen from the inside, in the other from without); again, as in *Lear,* the two ways are dialectically opposed. In the play the two aspects of choice are figured by Lear and Gloucester as two errors of the understanding, one active and the other passive. In the novel it is rather a plot of acceptance and refusal; the way of acceptance is art and the way of refusal is, in some guise, love. From the first pages of the book the two imperious callings dispute for the soul of the hero and his counterpart.

Although Swann thinks and feels and loves in a manner which makes him kin to the narrator, this basic similarity of temperaments only emphasizes the radical difference of their two choices. It is Swann who first introduces the narrator to the world of art, just as his daughter introduces him to the world of love. Swann, who cannot profit from his own experience with Odette, is to become for the narrator a kind of *Schwanung,* a presentiment and a warning. Unlike the narrator he cannot see the dialectical corollary to the world of vertiginous change which he discovers behind the moods and appearances of the beloved; the corollary is clearly his own discontinuity. Like the narrator he cherishes some of the same art objects, and like him thinks by vital analogy and similitude. But unlike the narrator at the end of his journey, Swann chooses to enlist the world of art and its message into the service of love. He converts the *petite phrase* of Vinteuil, which calls to him from that world, into the "national anthem" of his love affair with Odette de Crécy. He tries to find in the world of flux the stability of a painting by Botticelli.

In external circumstance or physical appearance the Baron de Charlus bears little similarity to Charles Swann. Yet in their gifts of sensibility and intelligence, more especially in their ways of responding to art and love, they betray an intimate identity. Between them they suggest the range of object and similarity of mechanism which Proust finds in his analysis of the centrifugal force of desire. Both men respond quickly to the stimulus of art, but both pervert its message. Just as Swann demeans the music of Vinteuil by involving it in his affair with Odette (so that eventually the *petite phrase* "says nothing to

him"), so Charlus, amateur of Balzac, confuses the events and characters of a fictional world with his own—and disastrously puts his faith
in the reality of the latter. He casts himself as Vautrin, as Baron Hulot,
even as Diane de Cadignan. In the revealing conversation between
Charlus and the members of the clan on the "little train," Balzac
becomes the mediator for Charlus's own predilections and obliquities.
He waxes eloquent on what he calls the "grandes fresques" of Balzac,
such as the *Illusions perdues—Splendeurs et misères:*

> It's magnificent, the moment when Carlos Herrera asks the
> name of the chateau past which he is driving, and it turns
> out to be Rastignac, the home of the young man he used to
> love. And then the Abbé falls into a reverie which Swann
> once called, very eloquently, the *Tristesse d'Olympio of
> pederasty*. And the death of Lucien! I no longer remember
> what man of taste, when he was asked what event in his life
> had most deeply pained him, replied: "The death of Lucien
> de Rubempré in *Splendeurs et misères*."

M. Charlus's "man of taste" was Oscar Wilde, and the Baron shares
with him both the identification with Vautrin and the desire to be an
"artist of life." And through the pursuit of the world and its
illusions both Charlus and Wilde are ultimately brought to a lover's
martyrdom.

During his discussion of Balzac, the Baron further identifies himself with Swann while enlisting him as an authority. Like Charlus and
Wilde, Swann has played the artist of life. All three are guilty of the
same error for which Proust (in the *Contre Sainte-Beuve*) indicts Balzac
himself, the confusion of life and art. Unlike Balzac and Wilde, Swann
and Charlus have faith without works. The narrator remarks toward
the end of Charlus's discourse:

> But the Baron was an artist to his finger tips! And now that
> he had begun to identify his own position with that de-
> scribed by Balzac, he took refuge, in a sense, in the tale. . . .
> He had the consolation of finding in his own anxiety what
> Swann . . . would have called something "quite Balzacian."
> The identification with the Princess de Cadignan had been
> simplified for M. de Charlus by virtue of the mental trans-
> position which was becoming habitual with him and of
> which he had already furnished several examples.

The parallelism of Swann's career and choice with those of Charlus is further reinforced by the skillful articulation of details of plot. The Baron is associated in the narrator's mind with his childhood memories of Tansonville as the "gentleman in twill," friend of Swann and an ambiguous admirer of Odette. The great soirée at the Princess de Guermantes' in *Sodome et Gomorrhe I* marks the point when Charlus inherits Swann's legacy, the point where the former comes to the center of the stage and the latter vanishes into the wings. Even the downfall in love of each, the moment of rejection, is engineered by the same hostess, Mme Verdurin, largely because of her jealousy for the same rival, Mme de Guermantes. Finally, the same musical theme (although radically transformed) orchestrates both events.

Proustian Space

Georges Poulet

In terms of the title it bears, one knows that the Proustian novel is very exactly a "search for lost time." A being sets out in quest of his past, makes every effort to rediscover his preceding existence. Thus one sees the hero awakening in the middle of the night and asking himself to what epoch of his life there is attached this moment in which he recovers consciousness. This is a moment totally deprived of any connection with the rest of duration, a moment suspended in itself, and profoundly anguished, because the one who lives it does not literally know *when* he lives. Lost in time, he is reduced to an entirely momentary life.

But the ignorance of this awakened sleeper is much graver than it seems. If he does not know *when* he lives, he no longer knows *where* he lives. His ignorance is no less important as to his position in space than as to his position in duration: "And when I awakened in the middle of the night, as I was *ignorant as to where I found myself,* I did not know in the first instant who I was."

The first question that comes to the lips of the Proustian being is, then, no different from that posed at the end by so many of the characters of Marivaux, fallen, as they recognize it willingly, from the moon, and asking themselves in what place and in what moment they find themselves: "I am lost," they say; "my head spins; where am I?" These heedless and charming people do not know where they are; they are all astray, because, in their distraction or their passion, they have lost touch with the world that was theirs. Or, rather—we are on a tragic plane, and in a way of life that hardly resembles Marivaudian heedlessness—the ignorance of the Proustian person is more precisely comparable to the state of mind of that being which Pascal imagines transported, while sleeping, to a desert isle, and awaking there in the morning, in terror, "not knowing where he is, nor the means of getting out."

The being who awakes and who, upon awaking, recovers consciousness of his existence, recovers also consciousness of a span of life singularly and tragically shrunken. Who is he? He no longer knows, and he no longer knows because he has lost the means of relating the place and the moment in which he now lives to all the other places and moments of his former existence. His thought stumbles between times and between places. This moment in which he breathes, is it contiguous to a moment of his infancy, his adolescence, his adulthood? The place where he is, what is it? Is it his bedroom in Combray, or Paris, or one of those hotel rooms, grimmest of all, because, lacking all habitual sympathy with the being who occupies them, they are not real places, they hold nothing personal; they are, so to speak, anywhere in space? On the other hand, for him who awakes in the night, how can he be sure how the place disposes itself? "For an instant," writes Proust in the preface to *Contre Sainte-Beuve,* "I was like those sleepers who on awaking in the night do not know where they find themselves, do not know in what bed, in what house, in what place on earth, in what year of their life they find themselves." Thus, groping, the mind seeks to situate itself. But it has "lost the plan of the place where it finds itself." At random, in the dark, one places the window here, on the opposite side the door; up until the moment when there comes a ray of light, which, making the room clearer, constrains the window to leave its place and to be replaced by the door. So that as chance directs, the order of places rotates and realigns itself from bottom to top. Or as it happened in another episode, in the very same place where the wall of his room rose, the hero, still a child, sees another space appear, a moor on which a horseman rides. But the first space is not abolished; the body of the horseman coincides with the doorknob. Two spaces can then superimpose themselves, the one on the other, as if there were "a wavering and momentary stained window." Now this vacillation, this vertigo, how many times has one not seen it affect the Proustian personage! It comes even when, being fully awake, he is disturbed by an unexpected event. For example, when at the end of an invitation Marcel reads the unhoped-for signature of Gilberte, he cannot believe his eyes; he does not know where he is: "With a vertiginous swiftness this improbable signature played at puss in the corner with my bed, with my chimney, with my wall. *I saw everything waver,* as does someone who falls from a horse."

Wavering of the wall where the child sees Golo astride a horse; wavering of the room where the adolescent receives the first mark of interest from his loved one; wavering, finally, of the room in which the anguished adult awakens in the night. Here are three examples of a dizziness, both interior and exterior, psychical and spatial, which, in three distinct epochs of his existence, affects at one and the same time the mind of the hero and the very places where he finds himself in these three moments. But these moments of vertigo are not the only ones. One remembers the singular episode of the three trees on the way to Hudimesnil. Strange and familiar, never before seen, and yet similar to some image of the past the mind cannot identify again, the paramnesic phenomenon experienced by the mind forbids the thought "to recognize them in the place from which they seemed, so to speak, detached," as well, moreover, to situate them in some other place; so that, adds Proust, "my mind having stumbled between some far off year and the present moment, *the environs of Balbec were wavering.*"

What wavers here is not only time but place. It is space. A place tries to substitute itself for another place; to take its place. It is the same in an episode even more memorable. At the end of *Le Temps retrouvé,* at the house of the Prince of Guermantes, the hero touches his lips with a strongly starched napkin. At once, he says, there surges the dining room at Balbec, "trying to shake the solidity of the House of Guermantes," and "making for an instant all the armchairs waver around me." In a word, just as the bedroom at Combray and the landscape of Golo on horseback, Balbec and the Hotel de Guermantes are vacillating and substitutionable. As do the wall and the moor, they contend for the same place. They are one too many; one usurps the place of the other. The phenomenon of Proustian memory has then not only the effect of making the mind totter between two distinct epochs; it forces it to choose between two mutually incompatible places. The resurrection of the past, says Proust in substance, forces our mind to "oscillate" between years long past and the present time "in the dizziness of an uncertainty like that which one experiences sometimes before an ineffable vision at the moment of going to sleep."

At the moment of going to sleep, at the inverse and corresponding moment of awaking, in the chiaroscuro wherein the consciousness is less prepared to withstand the phenomena that trouble it, the Proustian personage sometimes sees space split up, divided in two, losing its apparent simplicity and immobility. And it can be that this experience should have, for him who experiences it, a vertiginous happiness. But most of the time, the discovery of the unstable character of places inspires in him, completely on the contrary, a feeling of apprehension and even of horror: "Perhaps the immobility of things about us," writes Proust, "is imposed by our certainty that they are themselves and not others, by the immobility of our thought in face of them. The fact remains that each time I awoke thus, my mind agitating itself, in order to find out, without succeeding, where I was, everything was whirling about me, in the dark: things, countries, years."

"Trying to know where I was. . . ." We see clearly then, from the first moment—one could almost say also: from the first *place*—in the account, the work of Proust asserts itself as a search not only for lost time, but also for lost space. The one is like the other, lost in the same manner, in the sense one says he has lost his way and looks for his road. But lost also in the sense one says he has lost his baggage, lost like the beads of a necklace that is broken. How to string together again the place where one is, the moment when one lives, to all the other moments and places that are scattered all along a vast expanse? One could say that space is a sort of undeterminable milieu where places wander in the same fashion that in cosmic space the planets wander. Yet the movement of the planets is calculable. But how does one calculate the movement of places that are wandering? Space does not frame them; it does not assign them one unchangeable position. As happens sometimes in the images of our thought, nothing contests the fact, says Proust, that a piece of landscape brought to the shore of today, "detaches itself so completely from everything, that it floats uncertain in my thought like a flowering Delos, without my being able to say from what country, from what time—perhaps, very simply, from what dream—it comes."

Delight of seeing the image of a place of which we cannot determine the origin moves in our mind, like a beautiful ship without a home port. But most often anguish, the anguish of seeing the mobility of places aggravate still more the mobility, already so frightening in itself, of our being. For how is one not to lose his faith in life, when he perceives that the only fixity he believed he found there—a fixity of places, a fixity of objects that are situated there—is illusory? The mobility of places takes away our last shelter. It raises our anchor. To what we are able to cling, if, like times and like beings, places are also swept on in this course that can lead only to death?

Finally, the mobility of places has as a consequence the respective isolation of these places, the ones in relation to the others. If places move about, unless they do so at the same speed and go in the same direction (but alas! we know on the contrary that their courses are essentially aberrant!) forcibly there must change also the apparently constant relationships that linked them to other places and that made of space a network of stable correspondences and proportions. The distance from Paris to Balbec varies; that from Balbec to Raspelière also. In brief, the absence or the reinforcing of habits, the attention or the distraction, the fear or the confidence, or, more simply, the substitution of one mode of locomotion for another, sometimes lengthens and sometimes shortens the roads we travel. But also, now and then, a more serious thing, there is no longer any road; the place where one is leads to no other places; it is like an island, isolated on all sides, incapable of prolonging the network of its vanished communications. A place broken off from the rest of the world, which subsists in itself and of itself, like a besieged citadel; a place situated in absence, as a negation or a lack of access to other places; a place that finally seems absolutely *lost* in the solitude of space: "Having no more any universe, nor any bedroom, nor body, except threatened by the enemies which were surrounding me, except invaded to the bone by fever, I was alone; I wanted to die."

The being bereft of place is deprived of a universe, without a fireside, without fire and abode. He is, so to speak, nowhere; or rather, he is it matters not where; a sort of floating waif in the emptiness of hollow waves. But also, what joy, what relief for him, when all at once his vertigo ceases, the walls stop turning around and around, the floating images regain their habitual fixity! Twice, in Proust's novel, there occurs an episode in which the author has exactly transposed, in the realm of space, this victory over the destructive forces of time, which precisely in its essence constitutes the novel. There is first the account of a familiar walk at Combray, where everyone except the father has lost the sense of orientation, so that, like an awakened sleeper, nobody knows where he is. But then, just at the moment when anguish should begin, and the uneasy question of the stray one: Where am I? is ready to spring to his lips, the author, through the mediation of the father, consents this time to express a reassuring answer: "Suddenly my father stopped and asked my mother: 'Where are we?' Exhausted by the walk, but proud of him, she confessed to him tenderly that she had no idea at all. He would shrug his shoulders and laugh. Then, as if he had brought it from his vest pocket with his key, he would point right in front of us to the little gate of our back garden, which had come with the corner of the Street of the Holy Spirit, to wait for us at the end of these unknown paths."

If familiar places can then sometimes give us up, they can also come back to us, and, to our great relief, can reoccupy their earlier site. As can be seen, these places behave exactly as the moments of the past, as memories. They leave; they return. And in the same way as in certain epochs of our existence, suddenly, without cause, without voluntary effort on our part, we regain lost time; just so, in the same apparently fortuitous fashion, thanks to the intervention of some providence or other, the person, wandering as he was in space, finds himself at home, and regains, at the same time, his lost place.

Thus we must pay particular attention to a second episode of the same kind, which, according to his method, Proust has placed further on in his book, in order to recall and deepen what has already been cited.

In the course of a musical evening at Madame Verdurin's, the young hero finds himself astray amidst a music entirely new to him in the heart of a country whose paths he does not know: "The concert began. I did not know what they were playing; I found myself in an unknown country. Where could I situate it? In the work of what composer did I find myself?"

Then, like a genie or a fairy from the *Thousand and One Nights*, whose benevolent intervention would dissipate the uncertainties of the listener, or like the father, who, during the walk in Combray, would reassure and inform his lost family, a magic apparition, says Proust, comes to assist the hero and to answer the implicit question he had asked. Now let us listen carefully to the terms in which the author retraces for us this conjuncture: "As when, in a country one does not claim to know, and where in fact one has arrived from a new direction, after having turned up a new road, one finds oneself all at once emerging onto another whose even the lesser nooks are familiar, but only one hasn't the habit of traveling there, one suddenly says to oneself: 'But it is the little path that leads to the little gate of the garden of my friends. I am two minutes from their place'; Thus, suddenly, I recognized myself in the midst of this music that was new to me. I was in the middle of Vinteuil's Sonata.''

Is there any need to hold that the similitude between those two passages can only be intended by the author? Too many details are alike, up to the little gate that opens into the garden of Aunt Léonie, and that of certain friends. No doubt, in the first of these two passages, it is a question of persons lost in exterior space; in the other, it is a question of a being lost in the midst of an interior space. But in the one case, just as in the other, the essential issue is the discovery of place. To discover the little gate at the end of the garden is to discover a place that is no longer drifting in space, but that has its place in our memories, and that bears a name. The person who was lost somewhere in the universe discovers himself abruptly in a familiar territory where nothing has changed. To find again the lost place is then, if not the same thing, at least something very similar to recovering lost time. When in the depth of memory, some image of the past offers itself confusedly to the consciousness, there still remains a task to be accomplished: which consists, says Proust, "in learning what particular circumstance, what epoch of the past is in question." This task bears a name. It is called *localization*. Now, in the same way that the mind localizes a remembered image in duration, it localizes it in space. It is not only a certain period of its childhood that the Proustian being sees rise up from his cup of tea; it is also a room, a church, a town, a solid topographical whole, which no longer wanders, which no longer wavers.

Whether it be by grace of memory, by an act of the imagination, or simply by reason of the faith by which we attach ourselves to certain sites, the latter are set to differ from all the others; they stand apart in the spaces of our mind. Places found again in the depth of our memory; places created in us by our dreams, or by participation in the dreamings of others, which is one of the effects of art; or yet, but more rarely, places directly perceived by us in their particular beauty and enriched by the presence of a being who confers upon them something of his own individuality—with Proust, there is a diversity of places, unmingled with others, which seem to live within their frontiers an absolutely independent life. Such is their essential characteristic. From the external world to themselves, there is not this natural topographical continuity that is found everywhere between one place and other places. From the moment one perceives them, on the contrary, one gets the clear idea that they do not extend into the surrounding universe, that they are separate from it. There is, for example, not far from Raspelière a certain landscape of forest and shingles: "One instant, the denuded rocks by which I was surrounded, the sea, which one perceived through their clefts, *floated before my eyes like the fragments of another universe."*

Another universe, into whose enclosed space one penetrates, not only as one would pass from this to that point of ordinary space, but from a local manner of existing to a manner fundamentally different, or as, in withdrawing into oneself, one is transported from places forming part of the exterior world to those purely ideal places which have their reality only within our mind. And, indeed, in the case cited, that is precisely so, and in two distinct fashions, since it appears in the story that the place in question is nothing but a landscape, by means of which the painter Elstir was inspired of old to depict scenes of fabulous subjects that had strongly struck the imagination of our hero when he had seen them: "Their recollection brought the places where I found myself so far *from the real world,* that I would not have been surprised . . . if I had in the course of my walk come across a mythological personage."

Here then the placing apart of a fragment of space, its isolation in regard to the real world, is the result of art, but of an art seen again across memory. Poets and artists have the power of giving us access to "some marvelous sites, different from the rest of the world." And that not only in the general characteristics which these places present, but even in certain concrete details that make such a route, such a nook of a garden, such a bend of river "appear to us other and more beautiful than the rest of the world."

A miracle that music also produces, and that is effected by the little phrase of Vinteuil, when, by a play of perspectives, it allows itself to be glimpsed, unexpected and delightful, at the end of a whole sonorous development: "And as in those pictures of Pieter de Hooch, deepened by the narrow frame of a door half-opened, far away, of a different color, in the velvet softness of interposed light, the little phrase appeared dancing, pastoral, inserted, episodic, belonging to another world."

It sometimes happens that the place that sets itself in contrast to all others appears *beyond* the others, not, indeed, to continue them, but, on the contrary, to mark the quality that makes them belong to another world. But it is also possible that the privileged place, far from standing out against that which surrounds it, differs from it only by certain nuances, it is true, essential, informing us by this mingling of familiar and unhabitual traits, that it is used as intermediary between the world as we know it, and another world that is quite strange and far off. It is as if then the landscape—shall we say perceived or dreamed of?—went to make up a sort of avenue, which it sufficed simply to follow, in order to pass from one universe to the other, whether one passes from external perception to reminiscence, from tangible reality to imaginary space, or from objective verity to that of art.

There is an admirable example of this in a "landscape" in *Jean Santeuil,* where, in a movement very rare for him, the novelist addresses the reader:

> And you too, older than Jean, reader, of the enclosure of a garden situated on a height, have you not had sometimes the feeling that it was not only other fields, other trees that extended before you, but a certain country under its special sky? These few trees that came up to the enclosure you had been leaning on were like the real trees of the first plan of a panorama; they served as a *transition* between what you knew, the garden where you had come to visit, and that unreal, mysterious thing, a land that lay before you under the appearances of plains, developing richly in valleys, letting the light play upon itself. Here are still real things . . . but farther away there is something else.

Sometimes, then, there is opened before us a road that leaves our habitual places, but that, insidiously, without our being able to render a clear account of the place where it passes an invisible frontier, leads us toward other places situated outside of our universe. It is thus that the walk of the Guermantes way begins normally enough along the course of the Vivonne, but, for him who would pursue it up to the sources of this river, ends in a place no less abstract and ideal than the Gates of Hades. And thus it is again that the corridor in which the Prince of Saxe is engaged in order to join in her theater box his cousin Guermantes, seems to branch off from the banal place occupied by the hero, a witness to this conjuncture, on "an eventual passage toward a new world," and "to lead the way to marine grottoes, and to the mythological kingdom of the nymphs of waters."

A long time before Alain-Fournier, Proust had thus conceived the idea of an intermediary center connecting universes of different species. But different from Fournier, the intermediary center does not present itself in Proust in the form of a "real" road, uniting two determined points on the map. Let us rather say that with Proust this center or road is the topological representation of the very act by which the mind transports what it sees, and makes the objects of the real pass into the imaginary: "Elstir could look at a flower," writes Proust, "only if he transplanted it first into the interior garden where we are forced to live always."—Interior gardens where we transplant not only flowers, but also landscapes, the shape of human beings, and the very names they carry. Interior places, which are truly different from all others, because, like the church of Combray, they possess another dimension and because we can only represent them to ourselves across a certain depth of duration.

There is nothing less objective, then, than genuine Proustian places; genuine places, those which are invariably connected with certain human presences. There is never, in fact, with Proust, a place described without in the foreground, the profile of such or such a figure; in the same way that there never appears in Proust a figure without the presence of a framework ready to insert and support it. Invariably it is in a landscape minutely circumscribed that the Proustian personage shows itself for the first time.

From the moment it appears, this place, associating itself with him, gives him a note as distinct and recognizable as a Wagnerian *leitmotiv*. Yes, no doubt, in what follows the personage will reappear elsewhere. But he will not cease to be bound to the primitive site in our memory. It is of this that we are reminded from the very first moment; it is this that we see unfold, unfold promptly, in whatever spot the personage finds himself; as if he had been fixed in a painting more revealing than anything else, where he will always be showing up against the same background.

It is thus with all Proustian personages. How to recall, for example, Gilberte, or rather the image the hero has formed of her, if not under the aspect of a little girl, accompanied by an old gentleman, and silhouetting herself with him against the background of the cathedrals they visit by turn. "Most often now when I thought of her, *I saw her before the porch of a cathedral,* explaining to me the significance of the statues, and with a smile that spoke kindly of me, introducing me as her friend to Bergotte." How on the other hand, to imagine Saint-Loup or Albertine otherwise than against the marine landscape of

Balbec. "He came from the beach, and the sea, which filled up to mid-height the stained glass of the hall, *gave him a background against which he could detach himself full length.*" Thus there is fixed before our eyes, inserted in his context, the image of the future friend of Marcel. Now it is the same for the "young girls in flower," and for the principal one of these: Albertine. "It was to them that my thought was pleasantly suspended when I fancied I was thinking of some other thing, or of nothing. But when, not thinking at all, I thought of them, more unconsciously still, they formed for me the hilly and blue waves of the sea, the profile of a procession before the sea."

Profile of a group, profile of a single face: "Was she not in fact the young girl I had seen for the first time at Balbec under her flat beret with her eyes intent and laughing, mysterious still, *slim like a silhouette profiled upon the wave?*"

Whatever the images may be, ceaselessly denied and substituting themselves for each other, that she will present in succession, Albertine will not be able to obliterate this first image, fantastically cast off by her lover on a seascape of clouds and waves. First image; last image, or almost so. For not much time before vanishing, saying goodbye to him one evening, Albertine, he says, held out her hand to him with the abrupt motion she had used in those first times on the beach at Balbec: "This forgotten movement restored to the body to which it gave life the form of Albertine, which hardly knew me at all. It gave back to Albertine, ceremoniously under an air of abruptness, her first newness, her unknownness, and *even her true frame. I saw the sea behind that young girl.*"

Thus, for Proust, human beings appear located in certain places that give them support and outline, and that determine the perspective according to which one is allowed to see them. A singular thing, this novelist of interiority invariably obliges himself to present his personages (except for one central consciousness) under the aspect of exteriority. Human beings are silhouettes that are outlined, shapes that fall under one's gaze. But still that is not enough to say. Not only are the personages bound to their appearances; it is necessary that their appearances be tied to a local environment that frames them and serves them, so to speak, like a jewel box. To this first framework others will come to add themselves, or to substitute themselves, as time goes on. Thus the Proustian being will appear, by turn, in a series of sites; just like persons who make themselves into a series of portraits, where one sees them, with a background that is always different: for example, a garden in the country, a wall covered with bills, a drawing room, a station platform, etc. But if, with Proust, a person is always put in a place, he is never, or very rarely described *between* places. It is as if it depended upon a witnessing look, which watched him more often than not installed in one of the diverse spots, from the one to the other of which it is necessary to suppose that he is transported; without, for all that, the eye of the author being capable or desirous of following the movement by which he goes from the one to the other. So that what here is found only rarely revealed is the continuous progression of beings in their physical as in their moral life, the motives that impel them to abandon their old frameworks in order to give themselves new ones. In brief, the only images of themselves Proustian personages are permitted to offer us are similar to those photographs of the same person, of which our albums are full. Such a person in such an epoch of his life, and then in such another; such a person in the country, in the city, in evening dress, in lounging clothes. Each of these "photos" is rigorously determined by its framework; the whole is discontinuous. Nevertheless, the association of each person to a certain place on which he is profiled has for effect the conferring upon it, if not the continuity that it lacks, at least one aspect that is eminently concrete. Beings surround themselves with the places where they find themselves, the way one wraps oneself up in a garment that is at one and the same time a disguise and a characterization. Without places, beings would be only abstractions. It is places that make their image precise and that give them the necessary support, thanks to which we can assign them a place in our mental space, dream of them, and remember them.

Proustian persons never let themselves be evoked without their being accompanied by the image of sites that they have successively occupied. Sites, moreover, that are not necessarily only those where they have really appeared. For to the series of real places where the hero remembers to have seen them there is added the image of the places where—even before they were encountered in flesh and bone— the hero dreamed of seeing them.

Each being is thus placed by us, not only in one place, but in a system of places, of which certain ones are real, and others imaginary. This is true for Gilberte, for Albertine, for the Duchess of Guermantes:

> Each of the women I have known did rise at a different
> point of my life, set up as a divinity, as a local protectress,
> first in the midst of a landscape that was dreamed, whose

juxtaposition checkered my life and where I was pledged to imagine it; and afterwards seen from the side of memory, surrounded by sites where I had known her, of which she reminded me by staying attached to them. For if our life is vagabond, our memory is sedentary, and it is in vain that we dash forward; our memories, shored to places from which we detach ourselves, continue to pursue there their domestic life.

Infallibly, then, with Proust, in reality as in dream, persons and places are united. The Proustian imagination would not know how to conceive beings otherwise than in placing them against a local background that plays for them the part of foil and mirror. To evoke a human being, this act so simple, which is the first act of the novelist composing his work, is tantamount with Proust to rendering a form visible and putting it in a framework. It is a trick of mind veritably essential, and which, with Proust, can be noticed not only in his novels, but in his critical writings and ideological essays, and even in his correspondence.

It is thus that writing to the pretty actress Louisa de Mornand, then absent from Paris, Proust gives himself up to the pleasure of imagining her in the place where she spends her vacation: "How much I would love to walk with you in these streets of Blois, which must be for your beauty a charming framework. It is an old framework, a Renaissance framework. But it is also a new framework, since I have never seen you in it. And in new places, people we love seem to have some sort of renewal. To see your beautiful eyes reflect the light sky of Touraine, your exquisite shape stand out against the background of the old castle, would be more moving for me than to see you in another dress. This would be to see you in new attire."

So that, by the grace of a momentary association, the beautiful eyes, the exquisite shape of the actress receive from the surrounding landscape a supplementary charm. But the inverse is equally true. If the place enriches the being who is found there, the being confers on the place where it is found something of its own individuality. "Thus in the depths of a landscape palpitated the charm of a being. So, in a being, all of a landscape invested its poetry." This phrase from *Contre Sainte-Beuve* already defines and prefigures the reciprocity of exchanges, which, in *A la recherche du temps perdu,* occurs between persons and places. Sometimes it seems that the place has so much need of a being that it is ready to engender it, to draw it out of its own substance, by a creative act identical to the one by which emanate from it flowers, trees, stones, houses, all the objects that constitute or furnish it: "The passer-by who aroused my desire seemed to be no model whatsoever of this general type: woman, *but a natural and necessary product of this soil*." Sometimes, on the contrary, it is the human object that seems to need to complete or enlarge itself by becoming the central point of a geographic reality: "I always imagined, situated about the woman I loved the places I then desired the most . . . I would have wished that this would be she who made me visit them, who opened for me the access to an unknown world."

Place, then, opens out to receive woman; but the image of woman opens out also to receive place. Of this curious interdependence, at once topological and anthropological, the best example is certainly that of *names*. Family names, country names, one knows the immense role they play in the Proustian work, a role so great that entire parts of it receive their title from them, and in a sense, it would not be an exaggeration to consider the whole novel itself as one vast amplification on the influence exercised by names on the mind. But family names and especially noble family names have this particularity, of being at one and the same time the name of a place and the name of a person, and of amalgamating thus into one unique identity the two ingredients of which the Proustian imagination has need. Of this mental alchemy realized by the name there are in Proust numerous examples.

That of the Duchess of Guermantes: "The Duchess of Guermantes had seated herself. Her name, as it was accompanied by her title, added to her physical person her duchy, which projected itself around her, and made prevail the shady gold coolness of the Woods of Guermantes right in the middle of the drawing room, around the ottoman where she sat."

Besides the name of the Duchess, there is another name, less known in the novel, but hardly less evocative:

> The name of the Prince of Faffenheim-Munsterburg-Weiningen kept in the freedom with which its first syllables were—as one says in music—attacked, and in the stammering repetition that scanned them, the dash, the affected artlessness, the ungainly German "daintinesses" projected, like greenish branches, on the "Heim" of dark blue enamel, which dis-

played the mysteriousness of a Rhenish stained glass window behind the pale and delicately chiseled gildings of the German eighteenth century. This name contained among the various names from which it had been formed, that of a little German watering place where as a child I had been with my grandmother. . . . Thus, under the visor of the Prince of the Holy Empire, and of the equerry of Franconia, it was the face of a beloved land where often there froze for me the rays of the six o'clock sun that I saw.

The name is thus simultaneously individual and local. It is the name of country on the same grounds that it is the name of person and the name of family. But it is even more. Under the form of one of those phenomena which one uses to transport objective realities into the mental world, it is this original topological entity (issued from the fusion of a real site with the image of a person or of the history of a family) that is an unreal place, since it has no place in the external space; but subjectively real, since it is situated in the spaces of the mind: "It is still today one of great charms of titled families that they seem situated in a particular *corner* of earth, that their *name* is always a *name* of place, or that the name of their country seat (and it is again often the same) gives automatically to the imagination the impression of settled residence and at the same time the desire of travel. Each titled name contains in the colored space of its syllables a country house where, after a difficult road, arrival is sweet on a gay winter's evening."

What is most often the Proustian snobbery? A revery on place names and noble families. Thanks to the colors whose names enrich them, to the thousand nuances of concrete humanity, which, by the agency of names, come to give them a particular countenance; places are set to play in the imagination of men a role no different from precisely that played by human people. Their marvels and mysteries become personal marvels and mysteries. Bearers of a name that humanizes and individualizes them, they show themselves and disappear, hide certain secrets, inspire certain desires, unveil certain beauties. Thus places merit being the object of our admiring curiosity and even of our love: "Places are persons," Proust writes somewhere. And elsewhere he insists: "Names present persons—and towns, which we get used to believing individual, unique as persons, a confusing image that draws from their dazzling sonority or their shadow the color by which they are uniformly painted." One is reminded of the grand movement of desire and dream unlatched in the mind of the young hero of *A la recherche du temps perdu* by the perspective of a journey to Italy. An infinite power of suggestion is revealed in the names of Florence and Venice, endowing these still unknown cities with a crowd of particularities intensely individual, though quite imaginary. It is that the hero, as Proust says, is still at an age when "we believe with a profound faith in the originality and in the individual life of the place where we find ourselves."

Of the place where we find ourselves; of the place, so much more, of which we dream. If there is, in fact, something significant in the Proustian topology, it is indeed the insistence with which the novelist returns to the originality and individuality of the character that places present—as well indeed the places conceived by interpretative thought, as those perceived in sensible experience and reviewed later in the memory. "There is something individual in places," recognized Proust. And some lines later, he speaks of "landscapes with which sometimes the night, in its dreams, embrace him with an almost fantastic power."

"This *unique* thing that a place is. . . ." The charm of a place, then, in the last analysis, is the fact that it is itself and not another; that it possesses, as much as human beings do, this essential characteristic that is called uniqueness. Just as Swann is Swann, and Albertine, Albertine (in such a way that it would be the gravest error for him who would like to understand these persons to search out in them only the most general traits that they share with all other representatives of the human species) just as much so, Venice is Venice, and Florence, Florence; and if it is undeniable that these places are bound to other places, to Italy, to Europe, to space, this abstract liaison that exists between all the points of extension would not help us to penetrate what is exclusively Florentine in Florence, and what is exclusively Venetian in Venice. Each place reveals itself as the seat of an absolutely original reality. Each place has, so to speak, nothing in common with other places, even with those that adjoin it. In brief, the Proustian conception of the radical originality of places neglects precisely the only characteristic that would permit *knowing them together*: the fact that places participate in the same space, and are placed at a greater or lesser distance, the ones from the others, but always measurable, on the same map.

Places are not able to be reduced to pure localization in space, no more than Charlus and Norpois, Françoise and M. de Bréauté, the Duke of Guermantes and the Grandmother of Marcel are able to be regarded simply as interchangeable specimens of the human race. For beings are persons, and persons can be understood only through their own originality. Now one sees that it is the same with places. Places are islands in space, monads, in "minute universes set apart." And the sole generality that matters in them is not at all the anonymous generality that is found in all the points of extent, but the identity that is noticed between similar types of landscapes whose resemblance strikes us despite the distance, and offers us "the consistency of a particular type of pleasure and of almost a framework of existence."

Reading (Proust)

Paul de Man

Georges Poulet has taught us to consider, in *A la recherche du temps perdu*, the juxtaposition of different temporal layers rather than the unmediated experience of an identity, given or recovered by an act of consciousness (involuntary memory, proleptic projection, etc.). The specificity of Proust's novel would instead be grounded in the play between a prospective and a retrospective movement. This alternating motion resembles that of reading, or rather that of the rereading which the intricacy of every sentence as well as of the narrative network as a whole constantly forces upon us. Moreover, as Poulet describes it, the moment that marks the passage from "life" to writing corresponds to an act of reading that separates from the undifferentiated mass of facts and events, the distinctive elements susceptible of entering into the composition of a text. This occurs by means of a process of elision, transformation, and accentuation that bears a close resemblance to the practice of critical understanding. The intimate relationship between reading and criticism has become a commonplace of contemporary literary study.

What does *A la recherche du temps perdu* tell us about reading? I approach the question in the most literal and, in fact, naïve way possible by reading a passage that shows us Marcel engaged in the act of reading a novel. This procedure in fact begs the question, for we cannot *a priori* be certain to gain access to whatever Proust may have to

From *Allegories of Reading: Figural Language in Rousseau, Nietzsche, Rilke, and Proust.* © 1979 by Yale University. Yale University Press, 1979.

say about reading by way of such a reading of a scene of reading. The question is precisely whether a literary text is *about* that which it describes, represents, or states. If, even at the infinite distance of an ideal reading, the meaning *read* is destined to coincide with the meaning *stated*, then there would in fact be no real problem. All that would be left to do would be to allow oneself to be brought nearer to this ideal perfection by taking Marcel for our model. But if reading is truly problematic, if a nonconvergence between the stated meaning and its understanding may be suspected, then the sections in the novel that literally represent reading are not to be privileged. We may well have to look elsewhere, in Marcel's erotic, political, medical, or wordly experiences, to discover the distinctive structures of reading, or we may have to go further afield still and use a principle of selection that is no longer thematic. This circular difficulty should not, however, prevent us from questioning the passage on actual reading, if only to find out whether or not it does make paradigmatic claims for itself. The uncertainty as to whether this is indeed the case creates a mood of distrust which, as the later story of Marcel's relationship with Albertine makes clear, produces rather than paralyzes interpretative discourse. Reading has to begin in this unstable commixture of literalism and suspicion.

The main text on reading occurs early in the novel, in the first volume of *Du côté de chez Swann*. It stands out as distinctly marked in the narrative of "Combray" where it follows immediately upon the young Marcel's visit to his uncle, the first explicit example of his ritualistic initiation to the ambivalences of good and evil. The scene is set within a thematic of closeted and hidden spaces, the "temple of Venus" of Françoise's bower, the "dark and fresh" smelling closet in which Uncle Adolphe retires, which will engender a chain of associations that will articulate the entire middle part of the book, the "dark freshness" of the room in which Marcel will hide in order to read, the "little sentry-box" where he finds refuge when his grandmother orders him to go outside. The symbolic significance of this setting is summarized in the interiorized image of the mind as a "cradle at the bottom of which I remained sheltered, even in order to observe what was happening outside." The first section of the passage does not deal with reading; it is three pages later when Marcel will climb to his room with a book, and only when he has been sent into the garden will the principal and very systematically structured discourse on reading be allowed to develop. But this preliminary section is solidly linked to the main body of the passage by a transitional scene centered on the characters of Françoise and the kitchen maid who was the main figure in the first section: "While the kitchen maid—unwittingly making Françoise's superiority shine at its brightest, just as Error, by contrast, makes the triumph of Truth more dazzling—served coffee which, in my mother's judgment, was mere hot water and then carried to our rooms hot water that was barely tepid, I had stretched out on my bed, with a book." The allegorical pair of Truth and Error crowns a passage that will be particularly rich in rotating polarities. But here, in this context of comedy, the chain of substitutions in no way preserves the integrity of the point of origin: the tepid liquid is a lowly version of genuine hot water, itself a degraded substitute for coffee. The kitchen maid is only a pale reflection of Françoise; in substituting for truth, error degrades and outwears it, causing a sequence of lapses that threatens to contaminate the entire section. All the later polarities will have to be on the defensive when placed under the aegis of the initial antithesis between truth and error.

Thus reading is staged, from the beginning of the text, as a defensive motion in a dramatic contest of threats and defenses: it is an inner, sheltered place (bower, closet, room, cradle) that has to protect itself against the invasion of an outside world, but that nevertheless has to borrow from this world some of its properties. The inside room "tremblingly shelters . . . its transparent and fragile coolness from the afternoon sun." The inner world is unambiguously valorized as preferable to the outside, and a consistent series of attractive attributes are associated with the well-being of the enclosed space: *coolness*, the most desirable of qualities in this novel of the "solar myth" in which the barometer so often indicates fine weather, itself linked to the restorative *darkness* of shaded light (Marcel being never so happy as when he dwells in the shade of the vegetal world), and finally *tranquility*, without which no time would be available for contemplation. But Marcel cannot rest satisfied with these positive aspects of a sedentary solitude. The truly seductive force of the passage is revealed only when the confinement to the obscure, private existence of inward retreat turns out to be a highly effective strategy for the retrieval of all that seemed to have been sacrificed. The text asserts the possibility of recuperating, by an act of reading, all that the inner contemplation had discarded, the opposites of all the virtues necessary to its well-being: the *warmth* of the sun, its *light*, and even the *activity* that the restful immobility seemed to have definitively eliminated. Miraculously enriched by its antithetical properties, the "dark coolness" of the room thus acquires the light without which no reading would be possible, "the unmediated, actual, and persistent presence" of the summer warmth and finally even "the shock and the animation of a flood of activity [*un torrent d'activité*]." The narrator is able to assert, without seeming to be preposterous, that by staying and reading in his room, Marcel's imagination finds access to "the total spectacle of Summer," including the attractions of direct physical action, and that he possesses it much more effectively than if he had been actually present in an outside world that he then could only have known by bits and pieces.

Two apparently incompatible chains of connotations have thus been set up: one, engendered by the idea of "inside" space and governed by "imagination," possesses the qualities of coolness, tranquility, darkness as well as totality, whereas the other, linked to the "outside" and dependent on the "senses," is marked by the opposite qualities of warmth, activity, light, and fragmentation. These initially static polarities are put in circulation by means of a more or less hidden system of relays which allows the properties to enter into substitutions, exchanges, and crossings that appear to reconcile the incompatibilities of the inner with the outer would. Proust can affect such confidence in the persuasive power of his metaphors that he pushes stylistic defiance to the point of stating the assumed synthesis of light and dark in the incontrovertible language of numerical ratio: "The dark cool of my warm room was to the full sunlight of the street what the shadow is to the sunray, that is to say equally luminous." In a logic dominated by truth and error the equation is absurd, since it is the difference of luminosity that distinguishes between shadow and light: "that is to say [*c'est à dire*]" in the quotation is precisely what cannot be said. Yet the logic of sensation and of the imagination easily remains convinced of the accuracy of the passage and has not the least difficulty in accepting it as legitimate. One should ask how a blindness comes into being that allows for a statement in which truth and falsehood are completely subverted to be accepted as true without resistance. There seems to be no limit to what tropes can get away with.

Structures and relays of this kind, in which properties are substituted and exchanged, characterize tropological systems as being, at least in part, paradigmatic or metaphorical systems. Not surprisingly, therefore, this introductory passage on reading that was placed, from the beginning, under the auspices of the epistemological couple of

truth and error, also contains statements claiming the priority of metaphor in a binary system that opposes metaphor to metonymy. The
passage reflects on the modality of the sun's presence in the room: it is
first represented in visual terms by means of the metaphor of a "reflection of light which . . . succeeded in making its yellow wings appear
[behind the blinds], and remained motionless . . . poised like a butter-
fly"; then in aural terms by the resonance of "blows struck . . . against
the dusty crates" in the street, and finally, still in aural terms, by the
buzzing of the flies, generalized into "the chamber music of summer."
The crossing of sensory attributes in synaesthesia is only a special case
of a more general pattern of substitution that all tropes have in common. It is the result of an exchange of properties made possible by a
proximity or an analogy so close and intimate that it allows the one to
substitute for the other without revealing the difference necessarily
introduced by the substitution. The relational link between the two
entities involved in the exchange then becomes so strong that it can
be called necessary: there could be no summer without flies, no
flies without summer. The "necessary link" that unites flies and
summer is natural, genetic, unbreakable; although the flies are only
one minute part of the total event designated by "summer," they
nevertheless partake of its most specific and total essence. The synecdoche that substitutes part for whole and whole for part is in fact a
metaphor, powerful enough to transform a temporal contiguity into
an infinite duration: "Born of the sunny days, resurrected only upon
their return, containing some of their essence, [the buzzing of the flies]
not only reawakens their image in our memory but certifies their
return, their actual, persistent, unmediated presence." Compared to
this compelling coherence, the contingency of a metonymy based only
on the casual encounter of two entities that could very well exist
in each other's absence would be entirely devoid of poetic power.
"The tune of human music [as opposed to the "natural" flies] heard
perchance during summertime" may be able to stimulate memory
in a mechanical way, but fails to lead to the totalizing stability
of metaphorical processes. If metonymy is distinguished from metaphor in terms of necessity and contingency (an interpretation of the
term that is not illegitimate), then metonymy is per definition unable
to create genuine links, whereas no one can doubt, thanks to the
butterflies, the resonance of the crates, and especially the "chamber
music" of the flies, of the presence of light and of warmth in the room.
On the level of sensation, metaphor can reconcile night and day in a

chiaroscuro that is entirely convincing. But the passage plays for higher stakes.

For it does not suffice for the sound of the flies to bring the outside light into the dark room; if it is to achieve totalization, the inwardness of the sheltered reader must also acquire the power of a concrete action. The mental process of reading extends the function of consciousness beyond that of mere passive perception; it must acquire a wider dimension and become an action. The light metaphors are powerless to achieve this: it will take the intervention of an analogical motion stemming from a different property, this time borrowed not from the warmth of the light but from the coolness of the water: "The dark coolness of my room . . . matched my repose which (thanks to the adventures narrated in my book, which stirred my tranquility) supported, like the quiet of a hand held motionless in the middle of a running brook, the shock and the animation of a flood of activity [mon repos . . . supportait, pareil au repos d'une main immobile au milieu d'une eau courante, le choc et l'animation d'un torrent d'activité]." The persuasive power of the passage depends on the play on the verb "supporter" which must be strong enough to be read not just as "tolerate" but as "support," suggesting that the repose is indeed the foundation, the ground that makes activity possible. Repose and action are to merge as intimately as the "necessary link" that ties the column to its pedestal.

The ethical investment in this seemingly innocent narrative description is in fact considerable enough to match the intricacy of the rhetorical strategy. For the burden of the text, among other things, is to reassure Marcel about his flight away from the "real" activity of the outer world. The guilty pleasures of solitude are made legitimate because they allow for a possession of the world at least as virile and complete as that of the hero whose adventures he is reading. Against the moral imperative speaking through the grandmother who "begs Marcel to go outside," Marcel must justify his refusal to give up his reading, together with all the more or less shameful pleasures that go with it. The passage on reading has to attempt the reconciliation between imagination and action and to resolve the ethical conflict that exists between them. If it were possible to transform the imaginary content of the fiction into actions performed by the reader, then the desire would be satisfied without leaving a residue of bad conscience. An ethical issue that is obviously involved in the success of the metaphor is connected to the central Proustian motive of guilt and betrayal

that governs the narrator's relationship to himself and to those united
to him by ties of love or affection. Guilt is always centered on reading
and on writing, which the novel so often evokes in somber tones. This
connection between metaphor and guilt is one of the recurrent themes
of autobiographical fiction.

One should not conclude that the subjective feelings of guilt
motivate the rhetorical strategies as causes determine effects. It is not
more legitimate to say that the ethical interests of the subject determine
the invention of figures than to say that the rhetorical potential of
language engenders the choice of guilt as theme; no one can decide
whether Proust invented metaphors because he felt guilty or whether
he had to declare himself guilty in order to find a use for his metaphors. Since the only irreducible "intention" of a text is that of its
constitution, the second hypothesis is in fact less unlikely than the first.
The problem has to be left suspended in its own indecision. But by
suggesting that the narrator, for whatever reason, may have a vested
interest in the success of his metaphors, one stresses their operational
effectiveness and maintains a certain critical vigilance with regard to
the promises that are being made as one passes from reading to action
by means of a mediating set of metaphors.

In this passage, the metaphorical relay occurs by way of the
flowing water: repose supports action "like the quiet of a hand, held
motionless in the middle of a running brook." In the sunny mood of
the text, the image is convincing enough: nothing could be more
attractive than this feeling of freshness rising from the clear water. But
coolness, it will be remembered, is one of the attributes of the "inner"
world, associated with shelter, bowers, and closed rooms. The analogical image of the hand is therefore not able to cross over, by its own
power, towards a life of action. The water carries with it the property
of coolness, but this quality, in the binary logic of the passage, belongs
to the imaginary world of reading. To gain access to action, the trope
should capture one of the properties that belongs to the antithetical
chain such as, for example, warmth. The cool repose of the hand
should be made compatible with the heat of action. This transfer
occurs, still within the space of a single sentence, when it is said that
repose supports *un torrent d'activité*. In French, this expression is not—or
is no longer—a metaphor but a cliché, a dead or sleeping metaphor
which has lost its literal connotations (in this case, the connotations
associated with the word *torrent*) and has only kept a proper meaning.
Torrent d'activité properly signifies a lot of activity, the quantity of

activity likely to agitate someone to the point of making him feel hot. The proper meaning converges with the connotation supplied, on the level of the signifier, by the "torride" ("hot") that one can choose to hear in *torrent*. Heat is therefore inscribed in the text in an underhand, secretive manner, thus linking the two antithetical series in one single chain that permits the exchange of incompatible qualities: if repose can be hot and active without however losing its distinctive virtue of tranquility, then the "real" activity can lose its fragmentary and dispersed quality, and become whole without having to be any less real.

The transfer is made seductive and convincing by a double-faced play on the cliché *torrent d'activité*. The neighboring image of flowing water (the hand suspended "in a running brook") reawakens, so to speak, the dozing metaphor which, in the cliché, had become the mere contiguity of two words (*torrent* and *activité*) syntagmatically joined by repeated usage and no longer by the constraints of meaning. *Torrent* functions in at least a double semantic register: in its reawakened literal sense, it relays and "translates" the property of coolness actually present in the water that covers the hand, whereas in its figural meaning it designates an amplitude of action suggestive of the contrary quality of heat.

The rhetorical structure of this part of the sentence ("repose . . . supported . . . the shock and the animation of a flood of activity") is therefore not simply metaphorical. It is at least doubly metonymic: first because the coupling of two terms, in a cliché, is not governed by the "necessary link" of a resemblance (and potential identity) rooted in a shared property, but dictated by the mere habit of proximity (of which Proust, elsewhere, has much to say), but also because the reanimation of the numbed figure takes place by means of a statement ("running brook") which happens to be close to it, without however this proximity being determined by a necessity that would exist on the level of transcendental meaning. To the contrary, the property stressed by the neighboring passage is precisely not the property that served in the coinage of the original metaphor, now degraded and become a cliché: the figure *torrent d'activité* is based on amplitude and not on coolness. This property functions in fact against the quality that the text desires.

The structure is typical of Proust's language throughout the novel. In a passage that abounds in successful and seductive metaphors and which, moreover, explicitly asserts the superior efficacy of metaphor over that of metonymy, persuasion is achieved by a figural play in which contingent figures of chance masquerade deceptively as figures of necessity. A literal and thematic reading that takes the value assertions of the text at their word would have to favor metaphor over metonymy as a means to satisfy a desire all the more tempting since it is paradoxical: the desire for a secluded reading that satisfies the ethical demands of action more effectively than actual deeds. Such a reading is put in question if one takes the rhetorical structure of the text into account.

The central text on reading develops in the wake of this initial complication. It has all the appearances of a set piece, so firmly constructed that it constantly attracts attention to its own system and invites representation by means of synoptic diagrams. The text follows "from inside to outside the layers simultaneously juxtaposed in [the] consciousness" of the reader. It extends the complexity of a single moment in time upon an axis oriented from maximum intimacy to the external world. This construct is not temporal, for it involves no duration. The diachrony of the passage, as the narrative moves from a center towards a periphery, is the spatial representation of a differential but complementary articulation within one single moment. For a novel that claims to be the narrative extension of one single moment of recollection, the passage undoubtedly has paradigmatic significance. The transposition of the present moment into a consecutive sequence would correspond to the act of fiction writing as the narration of the moment. This act would then be coextensive with the act of self-reading by means of which the narrator and the writer, now united in one, fully understand their present situation (including all its negative aspects) by means of the retrospective recapitulation of its genesis. Nor would it differ from the response available to the reader of *A la recherche du temps perdu* who, mediated by Proust's novel, understands the narrative voice as the dispenser of a true knowledge that also includes him. The "moment" and the "narration" would be complementary and symmetrical, specular reflections of each other that could be substituted without distortion. By an act of memory or of anticipation, the narrative can retrieve the full experience of the moment. We are back in the totalizing world of the metaphor. Narrative is the metaphor of the moment, as reading is the metaphor of writing.

The passage is indeed ordered around a central, unifying metaphor, the "single and unbending projection of all the forces of my life [même et infléchissable jaillissement de toutes les forces de ma vie]" within which the various levels of reading are said to constitute "sections at the different levels of an iridescent fountain that appeared to be motionless." The figure aims at the most demanding of reconciliations, that of motion and stasis, a synthesis that is also at stake in the model of narrative as the diachronic version of a single moment. The continuous flow (*jaillissement*) of the narrative represents an identity that is beyond the senses and beyond time as something accessible to sight and sensation and therefore comprehensible and articulated, just as the unique and timeless fascination of reading can be divided into consecutive layers shaped like the concentric rings of a tree trunk. Within a closed system of part and whole, the complementarity of the vertical juxtaposition and the horizontal succession is firmly established. With regard to the narrative, the proof of this complementarity will be the absence of interruptions, the lack of jagged edges which allows for the characterization of the novel's narrative texture as a play of fragmentation and reunification that can be called *fondu*, (i.e., smooth [Gérard Genette]) or *soudé*, (i.e., welded [Proust]). The continuity is not only apparent in the fluency of the transitions or in the numberless symmetries of the composition, but also in the strict coherence between meaning and structure. The passage is a persuasive case in point: to the stated assertion that reading is grounded in a firm relationship between inside and outside corresponds a text that is structured in a particularly rigorous and systematic way. But if the complementarity were to be an illusion, a very different story would ensue, more like the loss of entropy that occurs as one moves from Françoise's hot coffee to the kitchen maid's tepid shaving water.

The persuasive value of the passage depends on one's reading of the fountain as an entity which is both immobile and iridescent. The iridescence is prefigured a few pages earlier in the description of consciousness as a "shimmering screen [*un écran diapré*]." The miraculous interference of water and light in the refracted rainbow of the color spectrum makes its appearance throughout the novel, infallibly associated with the thematics of metaphor as totalization. It is the perfect analogon for the figure of complementarity, the differences that make up the parts absorbed in the unity of the whole as the colors of the spectrum are absorbed in the original white light. The solar myth of *A la recherche du temps perdu* would then be condensed in the scarf of Iris, as when the flower metaphors associated with girls and women are said to "appear at once on their two sides, like complementary colors." The "necessary link" between the imagined figure and its sensory qualities make it more seductive than the empirical, "real" landscape of Combray. Unlike this real landscape, the symbolic one is "a true part of Nature itself, worthy of study and meditation."

The superiority of the "symbolic" metaphor over the "literal," prosaic, metonymy is reasserted in terms of chance and necessity. Within the confines of the fiction, the relationship between the figures is indeed governed by the complementarity of the literal and the figural meaning of the metaphor. Yet the passage seems oddly unable to remain sheltered within this intratextual closure. The complementarity is first asserted with reference to the narrator's relationship to the landscape he inhabits, but it soon extends towards another binary set of themes, those of "love" and "voyage": "Therefore, if I always imagined, surrounding the woman I loved, the landscape I most keenly wished to see at that moment . . . it was not because a mere association of ideas existed between them. No, it is because my dreams of love and of travel were only moments—which I now artificially disentangle . . .—in the single and unbending projection of all the forces of my life." But what is here called "love" and "travel" are not, like the narrator and his natural setting, two intra-textual moments in a fiction, but rather the irresistible motion that forces any text beyond its limits and projects it towards an exterior referent. The movement coincides with the need for a meaning. Yet at the beginning of the passage Marcel has stated the impossibility for any consciousness to get outside itself, suggesting this very ideality, paradoxically enough, by means of an analogy derived from a physical phenomenon: "When I saw something external, my awareness of the fact that I was seeing it remained between the object and myself, bordering it as with a thin spiritual layer that prevented me from touching it directly; the object would evaporate, so to speak, before I could come into contact with it, just as a red-hot body that approaches a wet object is unable to touch its humidity, since it is always preceded by a zone of vapor." Three pages further on, it seems that the language of consciousness is unable to remain thus ensconced and that, like so many objects and so many moments in Proust's novel, it has to turn itself out and become the outer enveloping surface: "For if we have the impression of being constantly surrounded by our consciousness [âme], it is not as by an unmovable prison; much rather, we feel carried by it in a perpetual impulse to move beyond itself and to reach outside." The epistemological significance of this impulse is clearly stated when, a few paragraphs earlier, we heard of a "central belief . . . that made ceaseless motions from inside outward, toward the discovery of truth." Like Albertine, consciousness refuses to be captive and has to take flight and move abroad. This reversal by which the intratextual complementarity chooses to submit itself to the test of truth is caused by "the projection of all the forces of life."

Proust's novel leaves no doubt that this test must fail; numberless versions of this failure appear throughout the pages of the *Recherche*. In this section, it is stated without ambiguity: "We try to find again, in things that have thus become dear to us, the reflection that our consciousness [*âme*] has projected upon them; we are disappointed in discovering that, in their natural state, they lack the seduction that, in our imagination, they owed to the proximity of certain ideas." Banal when taken by itself, the observation acquires considerable negative power in context, when one notices that it occurs at the center of a passage whose thematic and rhetorical strategy it reduces to naught. For if the "proximity" between the thing and the idea of the thing fails to pass the test of truth, then it fails to acquire the complementary and totalizing power of metaphor and remains reduced to "the chance of a mere association of ideas." The co-presence of intra- and extratextual movements never reaches a synthesis. The relationship between the literal and the figural senses of a metaphor is always, in this sense, metonymic, though motivated by a constitutive tendency to pretend the opposite.

The image of the iridescent fountain is a clear case in point. Everything orients the trope towards the seduction of metaphor: the sensory attractiveness, the context, the affective connotations, all cooperate to this aim. As soon however as one follows Proust's own injunction to submit the reading to the polarity of truth and error (a gesture that can be repressed but never prevented), statements or strategies that tended to remain unnoticed become apparent and undo what the figure seemed to have accomplished. The shimmering of the fountain then becomes a much more disturbing movement, a vibration between truth and error that keeps the two readings from converging. The disjunction between the aesthetically responsive and the rhetorically aware reading, both equally compelling, undoes the pseudo-synthesis of inside and outside, time and space, container and content, part and whole, motion and stasis, self and understanding, writer and reader, metaphor and metonymy, that the text has constructed. It functions like an oxymoron, but since it signals a logical rather than a representational incompatibility, it is in fact an aporia. It designates the irrevocable occurrence of at least two mutually exclusive readings and asserts the impossibility of a true understanding, on the level of the figuration as well as of the themes.

The question remains whether by thus allowing the text to deconstruct its own metaphors one recaptures the actual movement of the novel and comes closer to the negative epistemology that would reveal its hidden meaning. Is this novel the allegorical narrative of its own deconstruction? Some of its most perceptive recent interpreters seem to think so when they assert, like Gilles Deleuze, the "powerful unity" of the *Recherche* despite its inherent fragmentation or, like Genette, stress the "solidity of the text" despite the perilous shuttle between metaphor and metonymy.

What is at stake is the possibility of including the contradictions of reading in a narrative that would be able to contain them. Such a narrative would have the universal significance of an allegory of reading. As the report of the contradictory interference of truth and error in the process of understanding, the allegory would no longer be subject to the destructive power of this complication. To the extent that it is not itself demonstrably false, the allegory of the play of truth and falsehood would ground the stability of the text.

One would have to untie the complex interlacing of truth and lie in *A la recherche du temps perdu* to decide whether or not the work corresponds to this model. But the passage on reading gives a first indication how such an analysis would have to proceed. It is preceded by an episode which deals, as by coincidence, with the question of allegory and which can serve as a warning for the difficulties that any attempt to reach an inclusive allegorical reading of the novel are bound to encounter. The passage consists of Marcel's meditation on the nickname "Giotto's Charity" by which Swann is accustomed to refer to the kitchen maid persecuted with such cruelty by Françoise, the cook.

Slave of a slave, pathetic emblem of servitude, the kitchen maid is first described as what one could call, with Goethe, *Dauer im Wechsel*, the element that remains permanent in the midst of change. She is characterized as "a permanent institution, whose unchanging attributes guaranteed an appearance of continuity and identity, beyond the succession of transitory forms in which she was incarnated." Swann, the personification of metaphor, is endowed with a particular knack for the discovery of resemblances, and he has observed the near-emblematic quality of this particular kitchen maid. She carries the "humble basket" of her pregnancy in a manner that, by its resemblance to the surcoat of the allegorical frescoes painted by Giotto in the Arena of Padua, reveals her universal essence. All the agonies and all the humiliations of the successive kitchen maids are concentrated in this particular trait of her physiognomy, thus raised to the level of an emblem. An allegory thus conceived is in no way distinguished from the structure of metaphor, of which it is in fact the most general version. In the same manner, metaphor warrants the identity of art as a "permanent institution" that transcends the singularity of its particular incarnations. What may appear surprising is that Proust selected servitude as the essence intended and reached by the figure. More surprising still, the allegorical figure that Swann's sagacity has singled out is Charity, a virtue whose relationship with servitude is not one of mere resemblance. By generalizing itself in its own allegory, the metaphor seems to have displaced its proper meaning.

Marcel, who has a more literary (that is to say, rhetorically less naïve) mind than Swann, has observed that the kitchen maid and Giotto's Charity resemble each other in still another way than physical shape. Their resemblance also has a dimension linked to reading and understanding, and in this capacity it is a curiously negative one. The property shared by the maid and by Charity is that of a nonunderstanding: both distinguish themselves by features they display "without seeming to understand their meaning." Both seem to be condemned to the same dyslexia.

The passage describes with great precision this shared inability to read. The allegorical image or icon has, on the one hand, a representational value and power: Charity represents a shape whose physical attributes connote a certain meaning. Moreover, it makes gestures or (in the case of a verbal icon that would no longer be pictorial) it tells tales that are particularly conspicuous in their intent to convey meaning. The figures have to be endowed with a semantic intensity that confers upon them a particularly effective representational function. The allegorical icon must attract attention; its semantic importance must be dramatized. Marcel insists that the kitchen maid and the Giotto frescoes resemble each other by their common claim to focus our attention on an allegorical detail: "Envy's attention—and, by the same token, our own—[is] entirely concentrated on the action of her lips" just as "with the poor kitchen maid, [one's] attention is ceaselessly brought back to her belly by the load that weighs it down." In a metaphor, the substitution of a figural for a literal designation engenders, by synthesis, a proper meaning that can remain implicit since it is constituted by the figure itself. But in allegory, as here described, it seems that the author has lost confidence in the effectiveness of the substitutive power generated by the resemblances: he states a proper meaning, directly or by way of an intratextual code or tradition, by using a literal sign which bears no resemblance to that meaning and which conveys, in its turn, a meaning that is proper to it but does not coincide with the proper meaning of the allegory. The facial expression of the "heavy and mannish" matron painted by Giotto connotes nothing charitable and even when, as in the case of Envy, one could perhaps detect a resemblance between the idea and the face of Envy, the stress falls on an iconic detail that sidetracks our attention and hides the potential resemblance from our eyes.

The relationship between the proper and the literal meaning of the allegory, which can be called "allegoreme" and "allegoresis" respectively (as one distinguishes between "noeme" and "noesis"), is not merely a relationship of noncoincidence. The semantic dissonance goes further. By concentrating the attention of Envy's beholder on the picturesque details of the image, he has, says Marcel, "no time for envious thoughts." Hence the didactic effectiveness of allegory since it makes one forget the vices it sets out to represent—a little as when Rousseau pretends to justify the theater because it distracts, for a while, vile seducers from their evil pursuits. It actually turns out that, in the case of Envy, the mind is distracted towards something even more threatening than vice, namely death. From the structural and rhetorical point of view, however, all that matters is that the allegorical representation leads towards a meaning that diverges from the initial meaning to the point of foreclosing its manifestation.

In the case of the allegorical figuration of Charity, things are even more specific, especially if one takes the origins of the passage into account. Proust does not start out from a direct encounter with Giotto's frescoes, but from Ruskin's commentary on Giotto's Vices and Virtues of Padua. The commentary is of considerable interest in many respects but it is especially striking in this context because it deals with an error of reading and interpretation. Ruskin describes Charity brandishing, in her left hand, an object that looks like a heart; he first assumes that the scene represents God giving his own charitable heart to her, but he corrects himself in a later note: "There is no doubt that I misread this action: she *gives* her heart to God, while she makes offerings to mankind." Ruskin also discusses the painter's ambivalent rhetoric, which is, he says, "quite literal in [its] meaning as well as figurative." Describing the same gesture, Marcel follows Ruskin's rectified reading but displaces the meaning by adding a comparison which, at first sight, appears quite incongruous: "she stretches her incandescent heart towards God or, better, she hands it over to him, as a cook would hand a corkscrew through a window of her basement to someone who asks for it at street level." The comparison seems to be chosen merely to stress the homely quality of the gesture, but one of its other functions is to bring about the reentry into the text of "the cook," that is to say, Françoise. The kitchen maid resembles Giotto's Charity, but it appears that the latter's gesture also makes her resemble Françoise. The first resemblance is not entirely unlikely: the sufferings of the hapless girl are vividly enough evoked to inspire a feeling of pity that could easily be confused with charity. But the further resemblance, with Françoise, is harder to understand: if the image, as a representation, also connotes Françoise, it widely misses its mark, for nothing could be less charitable than Françoise, especially in her attitude toward the kitchen maid. The neighboring episode which narrates in great detail the refinements of Françoise's methods of torture, makes very clear that the literal sense of this allegory treats its proper sense in a most uncharitable manner. The rhetorical interest of the section, which culminates in the tragicomic scene where Françoise is seen weeping hot tears upon reading, in a book, a description of the very symptoms that prompt her most savage violence when she literally encounters them in her slave, is that a single icon engenders two meanings, the one representational and literal, the other allegorical and "proper," and that the two meanings fight each other with the blind power of stupidity. With the complicity of the writer, the literal meaning obliterates the allegorical meaning; just as Marcel is by no means inclined to deprive himself of Françoise's services, so the writer has no intention of doing without the thematic powers of literal representation and, moreover, would not be able to do so if he tried.

In the ethical realm of Virtue and Vice, the ambivalences of the allegorical figure thus lead to strange confusions of value. And if one bears in mind that, in Proust's allegory of reading, the couple Françoise/ kitchen maid also enacts the polarity of truth and falsehood, then the epistemological consequences of the passage are equally troubling. Since any narrative is primarily the allegory of its own reading, it is caught in a difficult double bind. As long as it treats a theme (the discourse of a subject, the vocation of a writer, the constitution of a consciousness), it will always lead to the confrontation of incompatible meanings between which it is necessary but impossible to decide in terms of truth and error. If one of the readings is declared true, it will always be possible to undo it by means of the other; if it is decreed false, it will always be possible to demonstrate that it states the truth of its aberration. An interpretation of *A la recherche du temps perdu* which would understand the book as being the narrative of its own deconstruction would still operate on this level. Such an interpretation (which is indispensable) accounts for the textual coherence postulated by Genette, Deleuze, and by Marcel's own critical theories and, at the far end of its successive negations, it will recover the adequation between structure and statement on which any thematic reading depends. But when it is no longer a matter of allegorizing the crossing, or chiasmus, of two modes of reading but Reading itself, the difficulty brought to light by the passage on Giotto's Charity is much greater. A literal reading of Giotto's fresco would never have discovered what it meant, since all the represented properties point in a different direction. We know the meaning of the allegory only because Giotto, substituting writing for representation, spelled it out on the upper frame of his painting: *KARITAS*. We accede to the proper meaning by a direct act of reading, not by the oblique reading of the allegory. This literal reading is possible because the notion of charity, on this level of illusion, is considered to be a referential and empirical experience that is not confined to an intratextual system of relationships. The same does not apply to the allegorical representation of Reading which we now understand to be the irreducible component of any text. All that will be represented in such an allegory will deflect from the act of reading and block access to its understanding. The allegory of reading narrates the impossibility of reading. But this impossibility necessarily extends to the word "reading" which is thus deprived of any referential meaning whatsoever. Proust may well spell out all the letters of *LECTIO* on the frames of his stories (and the novel abounds in gestures aimed in that direction), but the word itself will never become clear, for according to the laws of Proust's own statement it is forever impossible to read Reading. Everything in this novel signifies something other than what it represents, be it love, consciousness, politics, art, sodomy, or gastronomy: it is always something else that is intended. It can be shown that the most adequate term to designate this "something else" is Reading. But one must at the same time "understand" that this word bars access, once and forever, to a meaning that yet can never cease to call out for its understanding.

The young Marcel is at first displeased by the discordance between the literal and the proper meaning of the allegory, but the maturity of his literary vocation is dated by his ability to come to admire it: "Later on, I understood that the uncanny attraction, the specific beauty of these frescoes was due to the prominent place taken up by the symbol, and that the fact that it was not represented symbolically (since the symbolized idea was not expressed) but as something real, actually experienced or materially handled, gave to the meaning of the work something more literal and more precise." This formulation, "plus tard, j'ai compris," is very familiar to readers of the *Recherche*, for it punctuates the entire novel like an incantation. Literary criticism has traditionally interpreted this "later on" as the moment of fulfillment of the literary and aesthetic vocation, the passage from experience to writing in the convergence of the narrator Marcel with the author Proust. In fact, the unbridgeable distance between the narrator, allegorical and therefore obliterating figure for the author, and Proust, is that the former can believe that this "later on" could ever be located in his own past. Marcel is never as far away from Proust as when the latter has him say: "Happy are those who have encountered truth before death and for whom, however close it may be, the hour of truth has rung before the hour of death." As a writer, Proust is the one who knows that the hour of truth, like the hour of death, never arrives on time, since what we call time is precisely truth's inability to coincide with itself. *A la recherche du temps perdu* narrates the flight of meaning, but this does not prevent its own meaning from being, incessantly, in flight.

The Depreciation of the Event

Richard Terdiman

Near the end of *Sodome et Gomorrhe,* Marcel leaves the Grand-Hôtel in Balbec to take the little train to La Raspelière, where Mme Verdurin is giving one of her summer parties:

> Ce qui me plasait dans ces dîners à la Raspelière, c'est . . . qu'ils "représentaient *un vrai voyage*," un voyage dont le charme me paraissait d'autant plus vif qu'il n'était pas son but à lui-même, qu'on n'y cherchait nullement le plaisir, celui-ci étant affecté à *la réunion vers laquelle on se rendait.*

> [The thing that pleased me about these dinners at La Raspelière was that . . . they "meant a real *journey*," a journey whose charm seemed all the greater to me because it was not an object in itself, and no one expected to find any particular pleasure in it, the pleasure being reserved for *the party we were bound for.*]

By this stage of the novel the reader, having experienced two thousand pages of Proust's manner, is acquainted with the kinds of scenes that habitually interest him. The *soirée mondaine* is part of a well-ingrained pattern of expectation, and Mme Verdurin and her guests are known quantities. All these elements seem to carry us, with the passengers in the little train, towards the next unfolding, at La Raspelière, of the ongoing tableau of society.

From *The Dialectics of Isolation: Self and Society in the French Novel from the Realists to Proust.* © 1976 by Yale University. Yale University Press, 1976.

135

The train trip (the *stations du "Transatlantique"*) lasts about sixty pages before the guests finally arrive at Douville, where they are met by the carriages Mme Verdurin has sent to pick them up. The next sentence is an extraordinary twenty-eight line period: one short ride from the station through the darkness until the term of all this created expectation is reached, "the brilliantly illuminated *salon* and dining room." But then, with a vertiginous movement, the tableau which seemed about to begin such a large expansion is snatched away and replaced by a disconcertingly summary snapshot: "tandis que les services nombreux et les vins fins allaient se succéder autour des hommes en frac et des femmes à demi décolletées [while the endless dishes and vintage wines followed one another amid men in evening clothes and women in low-cut gowns]." Suddenly the guests are out the door again and find themselves back in the little train riding home. In the course of this single sentence the soirée has simply evaporated.

The effect is treated with an almost total lack of emphasis and seems to carry no weight at all. Yet it is clear nonetheless that Proust has used the pattern of the train trip, counting off the stations one by one, to rouse the reader's anticipation of the conclusion of the voyage— the arrival at Douville—and the expansive party scene to follow. His *escamotage* of the evening at La Raspelière transforms Douville, which should have been the last stop, into nothing more than a point at which the travelers change trains.

The meaning of such an elaborate mystification becomes clear soon after the little train begins its shaky progress home. The pattern of the trip fits into a higher and more emotionally charged structure, the narrator's relationship with Albertine, and the real moment toward which the entire scene has been made to move without a glance in that direction is the revelation, just a few stops later, of Albertine's relations with Mlle Vinteuil and her lesbian friend. Albertine's words, "spoken as we entered the Parville station," crush the narrator, and reveal that Douville was only a decoy. The actual terminus of the train's rocking advance along the coast, a rhythm which has continued for more than eighty pages now, is Parville. By occupying the reader elsewhere Proust has left him as unprepared as Marcel for the sudden shock of a critical event.

Proust's freedom to manipulate events in *A la recherche du temps perdu* depends upon the insignificance of the event in his conception of narrative. The individuality of his conception is based on a series of patterns of deformation—for example the misdirection of attention in the scene just considered—which often characterizes his treatment of the tale. Not that there is any lack of real events in *La Recherche:* two dozen important deaths, including one or two possible suicides; half a dozen consequential marriages and corresponding noteworthy changes of identity; numerous liaisons and some shocking scandals; several meteoric rises and precipitous declines in the worlds of society and art; and assorted plots, intrigues, conflicts, rivalries, and crucial discoveries— all of these together might have provided the material of a stirring series of adventure novels.

That such animated happenings should finally provoke so little suspense before they arrive, produce so little agitation in their passing, and cause so little significant alteration in the manner of telling once they are known results from the systematic way Proust has chosen to devalue the dynamic element they contain. His techniques for doing so are considerably more effective than any seen in Flaubert. Their object, to be sure, is the same. Whereas in the Realist paradigm events were treated as the centers of intensity around which the story naturally organized itself, accentuating their passion, their drama, their inherent vigor, Proust arranges these marriages, deaths, intrigues and revelations to diminish the energy they would otherwise radiate. Their animation is diffused, sapped, hidden or otherwise denied wherever it threatens to irrupt into the center focus of the narration. The entire concept of the event, its seemingly irreducible singularity, its elemental hardness, and thereby its very authenticity are altered by these procedures.

It was not always so. The treatment of episodes such as Couzon's speech in the Chamber of Deputies in *Jean Santeuil* provides a norm against which the refusal of such procedures in corresponding passages of the later novel can be measured. Couzon's courageous protest against the Chamber's refusal to aid the victims of the Armenian massacre is a vigorous composition which makes the most of the melodrama of politics. The scene's beginning is cast in the present tense to achieve maximum reality of presentation: "He is at the rostrum and he waits, rocking back and forth like a boat ready to depart though not yet untied, but swinging in the current in anticipation. Once or twice he says, 'Messieurs!' His voice is strong, almost astonishing; an extraordinary degree of emotion makes it quiver and shift." Then the telling shifts to the preterite in order to emphasize the full singularity of the event: "With the suddenness of a shot after the trigger is pulled, the wild applause of the extreme Left answered him." The orator is there at the rostrum, the force of his emotion is felt by

Jean in the gallery and through him by the reader. At stake are the lives
of "two hundred thousand people." The suspense is exquisite, and
Couzon's sudden defeat by the majority's cloture vote is a shock
manipulated for maximum dramatic force. The entire scene lives by its
dynamism.

The *séance à la Chambre* in *A la recherche du temps perdu* is handled
to achieve quite a different effect. This time the center of attention is
the prominent député M. de Guermantes-Bouillon, Prince des Laumes—
the Duc de Guermantes in his youth—and the scene is presented as a
commented newspaper transcript of a rather puerile intervention by
the Prince, the subject of which, significantly, is never mentioned:
"The astonishment, I would not be exaggerating to say the stupor
(*strong reaction of approval from the Right*) I felt at hearing the words of
someone who is still, I presume, a member of the Government . . .
(*thunderous applause . . .*)" (Proust's italics). This is only the sham of
excitement. It remains intentionally hollow, for nothing is at stake
here. Meanwhile the narrator's cynical comments ("this 'thunderous
applause' breaks down the last shred of hesitation in the mind of the
commonsense reader") dismantle and devitalize the scene. It belongs to
the realm of satire rather than that of drama. In *A la recherche du temps
perdu* the absence of a connected political plot and the vagueness of the
political elements that remain are measures of the distance which
separates Proust's mature narrative conception from *Jean Santeuil*.

The essence of the Realist paradigm is its portrayal of the world as
a terrain for human action, as a frame for exploits by which men
attempt to affirm and transform themselves. The dynamic tone of
Realist narration—whose elemental form is the account of a concrete
event—is precisely what Proust tends to shun in creating the world of
La Recherche. Moreover, the *parti pris* against such narration is quite
conscious. As Proust says with regard to concrete reality: "Tout en
haut [de l'èchelle intellectuelle], ceux qui se sont fait une vie intérieure
ambiante ont peu égard à l'importance des événements [At the summit
(of the intellectual scale), those who have created for themselves an
interior life which occupies them pay little attention to the importance
of outside events]."

Of course, it is the shape an event takes in the telling, rather than
its bare existence, that determines its influence as an element in the
world of a novel. The events in *La Recherche* exhibit a strange diapha-
neity. Through the complex of techniques Proust devised to devalue
them, they come to lack the solidity that in our ordinary understand-

ing makes an event the fact it is. It is not easy to say when a Proustian event takes place, as Proust suggests in *La Prisonnière:* "Il semble que les événements soient plus vastes que le moment où ils ont lieu et ne peuvent y tenir tout entiers [Events seem vaster than the moment of their occurrence, and cannot be completely contained within it]." It seems that events in Proust have no fixed location in chronology. Since the narration is retrospective throughout *La Recherche,* the narrator is free at any point to upset timeline telling: "Moreover, let us jump ahead of events to state that." Such interventions are frequent.

Consider this passage from the earliest pages of the novel:

> Ou bien en dormant j'avais rejoint sans effort un âge à jamais révolu de ma vie primitive, retrouvé telle de mes terreurs enfantines comme celle que mon grand-oncle me tirât par mes boucles et qu'avait dissipée le jour—*date* pour moi d'*une ère* nouvelle—où on les avait coupées. J'avais oublié cet *événement* pendant mon sommeil, j'en retrouvais le souvenir aussitôt que j'avais réussi à m'éveiller pour échapper aux mains de mon grand-oncle, mais par mesure de précaution j'entourais complètement ma tête de mon oreiller avant de retourner dans le monde des rêves.

> [Or perhaps, while asleep, I would have returned effortlessly to an earlier stage of my life, forever gone, and experienced again one of my childhood terrors, such as my great-uncle's pulling my curls, which fear had been effectively dispelled on the day—the first *date* of a new *era* for me—when they had been cut off. I had forgotten that *event* during my sleep; but the memory came back as soon as I had succeeded in waking up to get away from my great-uncle; still, as a precaution, I would bury my head in my pillow before returning to the world of dreams.]

Concrete reality has no more prestige for Proust than it did for Huysmans. This passage makes the point through a rather tender humor, but its terms reveal how paradoxical the Proustian event can be. The narrator's thoughts are voyaging wildly through time as he emerges from sleep. He conflates several different ages, gently mocking rational chronology by describing the comic "mesure de précaution" of burying his head under the pillow to protect himself from something which ceased to be a threat many years before. Though it "took place" (as we naïvely say) perhaps twenty years previous, the "event"—the cutting of his hair—even now has not thoroughly happened.

In effect, a Proustian event occurs whenever the teller's memory falls upon it. The tendency is perceptible in the nineteenth-century tradition as the logic of the protagonist's mental associations increasingly becomes the logic of the tale. But by abandoning third-person narration with its external objective anchor in favor of the multiple "I" of his first-person, Proust freed the concrete event from rational chronology to a markedly greater degree. Proustian events diffuse through the texture of his narration. They hardly ever "occur."

A bit further on is a much more crucial incident, the "good night kiss." The narrator uses the same terms we have already seen to characterize its significance: "Il me semblait . . . que cette soirée commençait *une ère*, resterait comme une triste *date* [It seemed to me . . . that that evening began an *era*, would remain as a sad *date*]." But the subjective effects of such an event are only understood over the long term, and it is fair to say that for Marcel this particular event does not "occur" until three thousand pages later, when with infinitely greater lucidity he recalls it in the Prince de Guermantes's library on the afternoon of his revelation. Its "occurrence" in the early pages of *Swann* might almost be called fictitious, a pure anticipation by retrospective memory of something not realized until many years later. Yet from our point of view it has already been successfully enacted. The technique is constant. These "prerevelations" are one of the principal means Proust employs to diffuse the facticity of the event over time, space, and the even less measurable dimension of memory.

The most important pattern of prerevelation in *La Recherche* relates to the flight of Albertine. The following passage occurs about three hundred pages before Marcel first learns of her departure: " 'Doesn't all that noise from outside bother you?' she asked me. 'I like it myself. But you're such a light sleeper.' On the contrary, I could be a very heavy sleeper at times (as I have already said, but *the event which is to follow* [*l'événement qui va suivre*] obliges me to recall the fact here)." The phrase in italics refers, of course, to Albertine's disappearance, but its chronology (*qui va suivre*) is accurate only in the most nominal way. The *événement qui va suivre,* through systematic prerevelation, has already occurred a dozen times.

It comes into existence as early as our reading in a table of contents (or in the "Pour Paraître ensuite" of an earlier edition) the title of the volume to follow *La Prisonnière*. Already the shock of the *événement qui va suivre* is being diffused, and the treatment of the story of Albertine depends upon the irony that arises from the experience we are given, long before it "happens," of the shock which Marcel will receive. For us the event does not "take place"; it unfolds with our knowledge of it, and our sense of its authenticity depends hardly at all upon its appearance on the last page of *La Prisonnière*.

Thus in prerevelation, events flow backward to anticipate their accomplishment in the chronology of the story. But in *La Recherche* there is prolongation into the future as well as predisclosure in the past. Proust was conscious of this double projection. Events, he wrote, "débordent sur l'avenir par la mémoire que nous en gardons, mais ils demandent une place aussi dans le temps qui les précède [Events overflow into the future through our memory of them, but they also occupy a place in the time that precedes them]." The latter phenomenon is translated in the technique of prerevelation; the former, which seemed to Proust the key to his narrative originality, becomes the confrontation of ages that occurs in memory, creating a "passé qui ne se réalise pour nous . . . qu'après l'avenir [A past which we only realize after the future has come and gone]." This radiation of events diffuses even the most crucial of them along the entire timeline of the story. We experience them as increasingly ineluctable atmospheres rather than as moments of decisive occurrence. The prospective or retrospective evocation of an event in *La Recherche* leaves it everything except the clearcut causal precision that, outside the novel, defines events for us.

At the beginning of September 1922, Proust wrote Gaston Gallimard to assure him that "mon prochain volume: *La Prisonnière,* est tout à fait romanesque [My next volume, *La Prisonnière,* is full of action]." To be sure, the volume contains two portentous reversals in the lives of major characters: Charlus's "exécution" at the hands of Mme Verdurin, and Albertine's escape. But the dramatic energy of these events is sytematically drained away by the narrative procedures outlined above. Proust in his maturity had little use for the "romanesque" in novels. He expresses his disapprobation by having the Baron de Norpois deliver a sententious encomium of the very type of novel Proust wished to discredit—since we understand that whatever Norpois praises, the narrator condemns. For Norpois, "The novelist's job is to devise a good story and to edify his readers, not to fritter away his time etching frontispieces and tailpieces." The Baron thus criticizes Bergotte: "One never finds in his enervated works anything you might call a plot-line.

No action—or very little—and, above all, no range." This de-dramatization is precisely what drew the young Marcel to Bergotte, and conversely the "romanesque" elements in Bergotte's novels, the progress of the intrigue, were what satisfied him the least: "The passages in which his delight in his own writing was obvious [*les morceaux auxquels il se complaisait*] were the ones I preferred. . . . *I was disappointed when he resumed the thread of the story.*"

The consequence of these attitudes, the tendency of these techniques in Proust, is to depreciate the active mode of narration. The narrative event fades as an element of construction in *A la recherche du temps perdu,* and Proust consciously contrasts his own practice with the form of the traditional novel—what he calls the "sterile and worthless adventure novel." What results is a comfortable relaxation of the usual linear coherence of plot. Incidents which in natural occurrence form a tension-producing sequence are dissociated so that the element of suspense in them is eliminated. The techniques already outlined, plus several more (suspension, the "feint," the revelation *ex nihilo*) which remain to be discussed have parallel effects. Through their use, Proust sets adrift the temporality of a causal series. What dramatized forms a plot, de-dramatized in Proust's treatment is free to become a collection of expansive, virtually independent scenes.

The unimportance of the novel's frequent internal contradictions shows how relaxed chronology becomes in Proust. Events are mis-dated or mistakenly occur more than once, but it hardly seems to matter. The stay at Balbec seems to last about six months if we judge by internal indications; Proust tells us it lasted three. He twice contradicts the hour at which Swann is refused entry at Odette's although she is at home; and there are numerous other instances. We pass over these confusions because they in no way affect the progress of the intrigue. They have no plot significance. E. M. Forster once observed that in *The Newcomes* Thackeray "by a most monstrous blunder . . . killed Lady Farintosh's mother at one page and brought her to life at another." *La Recherche* reanimates at least fourteen different characters. But the extraordinarily low degree of contingence between events and existences makes it possible for characters in Proust to die a death which does not signify and profit from an absent-minded revitalization without inconveniencing anything or anyone in the world they leave and return to.

Proust dealt himself with his anachronisms, anticipations, and other sins against the calendar in a letter (August 6, 1922) to Benjamin

Crémieux, who had wondered about a possible error of chronology in the novel. The humorous simplicity of Proust's response reemphasizes the fact that, in the absence of a plot which lays crucial importance upon a time scheme precise to the minute, month, or even year, contradictions and confusions make no difference. So he simply dismissed the discrepancy Crémieux had questioned: "Einsteinisons-le si vous voulez pour plus de commodité [Let's 'Einsteinize' it to make things easier]."

In the active mode of narration, human actions which engage the characters' responsibility direct and pattern the course of the story. Proust's disinclination to exploit active narration makes *A la recherche du temps perdu* an extraordinarily unconstrained structure, and one guided by no coherent plot principle that we can abstract from its texture. A remark by Barbara Hardy concerning Tolstoy applies *a fortiori* to *La Recherche*. Ms. Hardy writes that the looseness of his form "may . . . help to explain why a novel by Tolstoy is for some people difficult to read and for many difficult to remember. There is not the clear diagrammatic pattern of decisive incident and decisive moral crisis to create constant tension, or to act as a useful, if reductive, pattern in memory."

A la recherche du temps perdu thus poses a real problem of attention for the reader. Proust recognized the difficulty—and in the main refused to do anything about it. We have seen the pains he took to ridicule attitudes (such as Norpois's) which called upon the writer to make the reader's job easier: "They said that the age of speed required rapidity in art. . . . They warned against fatiguing the audience's attention." But the complication of Proust's style of narration works here to his advantage. By declining the active mode of narration, Proust's manner obliges us to read with the kind of attention appropriate to the intricate meaning to be conveyed. In his 1913 interview with Elie-Joseph Bois, Proust was concerned that understanding of the book he was about to publish not be distorted by a style of reading appropriate to the kind of novel M. de Norpois enjoyed:

> *Du côté de chez Swann* n'est pas ce qu'on appelle un livre de chemin de fer, qu'on parcourt du coin de l'oeil et en sautant des pages, c'est un livre original, étrange même, profond, réclamant toute l'attention du lecteur, *mais la forçant aussi.* . . . D'action, de cette action qu'on est accoutumé de trouver dans la plupart des romans et qui vous emporte, plus ou

moins ému, à travers une série d'aventures jusqu'à ou dénouement fatal—*il n'y en a pas.*

[*Du côté de chez Swann* is not what one might call vacation reading, the kind of book you skim through with your mind on something else. This novel is original, even strange, profound, requiring all of the reader's attention, but *forcing him to give it.* . . . As for plot, the kind of plot we are accustomed to finding in the majority of novels, the kind that carries you emotionally away with it through a series of adventures to a tragic conclusion—*there is none.*]

In spite of this effort to prepare the audience, Proust suffered because his book was found so difficult to read. He never resigned himself to the fact that other writers gained much wider audiences simply because they had an easier manner, and complained sourly to Gallimard (3 December 1921): "*Nène* [a novel by Pérochon which had already sold 75,000 copies] is the rare case of a Goncourt Prize book which, rightly or wrongly, is thought of as a 'decent novel,' nothing extraordinary. The difference in publication figures between it and *Jeunes filles* [which had won the previous year's Goncourt] seems astonishing to me. Perhaps it's because *Nène* is *easier reading.*"

Though the judgment obviously hurt him, Proust was right. It seems undeniable that the most immediate emotion felt by readers of *La Recherche* is not astonishment, or admiration, but a peculiar tedium. With the suppression of the active mode, no other outcome was possible. To say this is not to depreciate Proust, it is simply to acknowledge one of the conditions of existence of Proustian form. His early admirers confessed the tedium with near unanimity, but pled intense compensating pleasures. As Maugham humorously put it, he "would sooner be bored by Proust than amused by any other writer."

A parallel exists between Maugham's witticism and a judgment of Wagner in *La Recherche.* The Duc de Guermantes has just enunciated one of his characteristic philistinisms: "Wagner puts me right to sleep." The Duchesse reprimands such ignorance: "You're quite wrong. . . . In spite of his intolerable longueurs, Wagner had genius." Her rebuke of Basin must have amused Proust. Though reduced to lowest critical terms, it represented a justification of his own manner (one imagines with discomfort how cutting Oriane would have been about the longueurs of *La Recherche*). But since we are obliged to admit the existence of Proust's tedium, we ought to consider how tedium functions in his novel.

In January 1921 Proust wrote to Gallimard to reassure him that the utility of his novel's "slow parts [*lenteurs*] . . . will become clear later on." Tedium is a favorable condition for the perception of telling in the synthetic mode. In the Realist paradigm, when we are bored, our attention (conditioned to anticipate the next element of the progression) immediately wanders, and the form's solidity collapses. But conditioned to respond to elements of expansion rather than elements of progression, our concentration is heightened as its object dilates, and we penetrate each moment with an ease that grows in proportion to our lack of concern with getting on. Proust's mockery of theories affirming that writers must not "fatigue the audience's attention" was coupled with a defense of his own practice. In the same passage, he continues: "as though we did not have at our disposal different kinds of attention, arousing the finest of which is precisely the artist's task." The "highest attention" for him was clearly the intensive, spreading concentration which obliges us to redefine Proust's tedium as a variety of entrancement.

An image in Walter Benjamin's essay "The Storyteller" (1936) captures the essence of much narration after Flaubert, and evokes the mood of Proust's novel with particular aptness. Benjamin writes: "Tedium is the dreambird that hatches the egg of experience." After belief that the hopes of the individual might be realized in the post-Revolutionary world collapsed, bringing the Realist novel down with it, the kind of literary entrancement that is described in Benjamin's image came to take on the role of a therapeutic compensation for the failure of real experience. Mallarmé had already insisted on the way literature had begun to outshine life. A passage from one of Maurice Blanchot's essays makes the connection explicit:

> Le monde de l'imaginaire tient entièrement lieu de réel, s'y substitue et l'efface: tel est . . . l'idéal de la lecture qui veut *prendre* le lecteur, l'envoûter, le réduire à sa seule condition de lecteur, qui en somme se veut à tel point passionnante qu'elle endorme celui qui s'y engage, qu'elle soit comme un sommeil sans réveil possible.

> [The imaginary world completely occupies the place of the real one, substitutes itself for it and obliterates it: this is . . . the quintessence of a kind of reading which desires to *take*

the reader, cast a spell on him, force him to become nothing but a reader; to be so completely fascinating that it lulls him to sleep with it; desires to become that sleep itself, from which no awakening is possible.]

The techniques which organize the narration of *La Recherche* to this end overturn virtually every aspect of the Realist paradigm. But for Proust's new fictional system to operate successfully the expectations of an audience accustomed to the traditional dramatic novel had to be forcefully redirected. Tedium is the most unmistakable sign of this redirection, and in this perspective, Proust's problem was not how to avoid tedium, but how, fruitfully, to create it.

The Self in/as Writing

David R. Ellison

The passage of the *Recherche* that stages most clearly the constitutive dynamics of Proustian selfhood occurs in the early pages of *La Prisonnière*: it is the episode in which Albertine "names" the protagonist. As I indicated toward the beginning of this chapter with reference to Genette and Lejeune, the sudden and unexpected emergence of the name "Marcel" is especially disconcerting in that it introduces into the text an element of modal uncertainty: it becomes difficult to determine whether we are reading a novel or an autobiography, a fiction or a confession. The appreciable merit of Genette and Lejeune consists of their careful respect for this ambivalence: both critics note that an autobiographical tonality merges here with the more pervasive "impersonal" narration of imagined events, thereby producing a hybrid textual form. Although neither Genette nor Lejeune does more than observe this fact in a general way, their contribution to Proust scholarship is nonetheless praiseworthy, for they are affirming that the existence of the word "Marcel" in the text is not the result of an authorial oversight or idiosyncracy, but a problem that demands interpretation. I propose, in the following development, to examine the paragraph on naming in its contextual setting and to establish a coherent problematics concerning the identity of the *je* whose articulated states of textual presence ultimately determine the applicability of the term *autobiography* to Proust's novel. I shall begin my analysis with a discussion of the Proustian

From *The Reading of Proust*. © 1984 by the Johns Hopkins University Press.

"double self" as it functions technically and thematically, before reading the passage on naming as such.

The best early study of the *Recherche* as autobiography is that of Hans-Robert Jauss, *Zeit und Erinnerung*. At a time when many critics had no vision of the novel as a totality, Jauss elaborated an interpretive grid that both respected the larger thematic movements and also included close analysis of images and symbols later to be taken up by Genette in a post-Saussurian, new-rhetorical terminology. The modern reader may feel a sense of estrangement in reading Jauss for two reasons: first, the latter's view of the novel as transformed "epic" may seem excessively literal in certain contexts; and secondly, the pervasive Hegelian terminology may seem somewhat out-of-date to readers for whom the implicit "referent" of deconstructive analyses has usually been the Hegelian system. Yet if we push Jauss a step further than he went in his interpretation, we discover to what extent the *Recherche* as novelistic form can be construed as a brilliant restatement of certain theoretical and methodological problems whose "answer" or working-out was the *Phenomenology of Mind*.

Jauss begins his study with the fundamental distinction between narrator ("das erinnernde ich," or "the remembering I") and "Marcel" ("das erinnerte ich," or "the remembered I"). He shows that this double register allows Proust to avoid the reductive tendencies of classical autobiography, in which a solidly established subject justifies his past from the retrospective and teleological point of view. It is to Jauss's credit to have demonstrated rigorously that the novelistic technique of Proust is inseparable from his aesthetic tenets. Most importantly, the time of remembrance (as revelation of involuntary memory) does not stand outside the textual development, but is integrated into remembered time: it becomes part of that temporal movement which Jauss has characterized as "futur dans le passé" (as opposed to the "passé du savoir" that defines *Les Confessions* of Rousseau or Goethe's *Dichtung und Wahrheit*). From Jauss's theoretical perspective, the "Overture" to the *Recherche* is not to be understood simply as a modern version of *in medias res,* but rather as the only logical way to begin a novel which, because of its double register, must begin in its middle, or, in other terms, must already have started. This we recognize as the problem of the Hegelian preface, though Jauss does not make the connection in an explicit way. In his "Vorrede" to the *Phenomenology of Mind,* Hegel explains that all attempts to situate his own work in an historical or intellectual context miss the mark or stray from the central

work of philosophy, which is to represent the truth in its progressive
unfolding, as the general which includes the particular:

> Denn wie und was von Philosophie in einer Vorrede zu
> sagen schicklich wäre,—etwa eine historische *Angabe* der
> Tendenz und des Standpunkts, des allgemeinen Inhalts und
> der Resultate, eine Verbindung von hin und her sprechenden
> Behauptungen und Verischerungen über das Wahre—kann
> nicht für die Art und Weise gelten, in der die philosophische
> Wahrheit darzustellen sei.

> Auch weil die Philosophie wesentlich im Elemente der
> Allgemein heit ist, die das Besondere in sich schliesst, so
> findet bei ihr mehr als bei andern Wissenschaften der Schein
> statt, als ob in dem Zwecke oder den letzten Resultaten die
> Sache selbst und sogar in ihrem vollkommenen Wesen
> ausgedrückt wäre, gegen welches die Ausführung eigentlich
> das Unwesentliche sei.

> [For whatever it might be suitable to state about philosophy
> in a preface—say, an historical sketch of the main drift and
> point of view, the general content and results, a string of
> desultory assertions and assurances about the truth—this
> cannot be accepted as the form and manner in which to
> expound philosophical truth.

> Moreover, because philosophy has its being essentially in
> the element of that universality which encloses the particular
> within it, the end or final result seems, in the case of philos-
> ophy more than in that of other sciences, to have absolutely
> expressed the complete fact in its very nature; contrasted
> with that the mere process of bringing it to light would
> seem, properly speaking, to have no essential significance.]

The achievement of Proust's "Overture" is to have effectively performed what Hegel explained in a discursive manner. The opening
pages of the *Recherche* show the coming-to-consciousness of a *je* who is
already observed by another *je*. What is confusion to the first is already
illuminated for the second self. Subjective consciousness is already its
own object; the text doubles into itself to produce its own temporal
progress. In this interiorized scheme of knowledge, *je* becomes itself in
a succession of ecstatic moments as the book demonstrates its (future)
coming-into-being.

For Jauss, the revelations of the Matinée Guermantes at the close of the novel create the aesthetic impression of a *temps incorporé* that Marcel discovers as he understands the deep identity between his past and present selves. Remembrance implies the continuity of an inner time, thereby presupposing a *moi permanent* in which "die Diskontinuität der *moi successifs* aufgehoben und zugleich bewahrt ist [the discontinuity of the successive selves is both negated and preserved]." The major assumption in Jauss's argumentation is that the successive selves of the protagonist, however discontinuous in their form of presentation, at least share the same essence. In rhetorical terms, we would say that the protagonist as "part" (momentary apparition) relates as metaphorical synecdoche to the narrator as "whole" (truth of the hero's falseness). Only this assumption will allow the Proustian system to function as a fluid progression.

The question that I would like to pose at this point, and then develop in a short analysis, is the following: can we safely suppose that the narrator relates to the protagonist as *Le Temps retrouvé* seems to affirm, or is the dual register of the *je* of a kind that does not allow for a Hegelian synthesis? I will now juxtapose the passage on naming from *La Prisonnière* to the well-known "Overture" of "Combray," which it resembles in many respects. The superposition of the two texts (in the strict geometrical sense) reveals a structural design that should help clarify the function and limits of the autobiographical mode in Proust's writing.

The pages leading up to the paragraph on naming thematize the double nature of Albertine: they compress into a series of quick and violent alternations the polar oppositions of virtue and vice, organic plant-object and disseminated, irrecuperable energy, that run throughout *La Prisonnière*. At first, the narrator emphasizes Albertine's fugitive tendencies and reflects on the difficulty of immobilizing a being whose desires remain forever unknowable. He even states that whatever identity one may wish to assign her implies a false stability "que nous lui prêtons [et qui] n'est que fictive et pour la commodité du langage." This observation gains in irony as the text progresses, but for the moment we see especially its function as generalization or law: how indeed can Albertine be granted identity if her inner self contains the contradictory double presence of beauty (aesthetic harmony) and of satanic evil? Moving inexplicably from the status of "rose jeune fille" to that of "lubrique Furie," she escapes categorization as she defies possession. Yet without the shadow of a transition, the narrator describes her also as the opposite of the creature of duplicity just evoked. Suddenly, we are told in a straightforward declaration: "Nos rapports étaient d'une simplicité qui les rendaient reposants." No longer a threatening force whose inner core eludes understanding, she is now an empty vessel in, through, and beyond which Marcel can supply his own peaceful dreams. He sees her as an apparition who reawakens in him the forgotten seascapes of Balbec: "Derrière cette jeune fille, comme derrière la lumière pourprée qui tombait aux pieds de mes rideaux à Balbec pendant qu'éclatait le concert des musiciens, se nacraient les ondulations bleuâtres de la mer." Later on, Albertine becomes a "plant" whose every movement "belongs" to Marcel: as plant, as poetic object, "son moi ne s'échappait pas à tous moments, comme quand nous causions, par les issues de la pensée inavouée et du re-gard." The short passage preceding the naming of the protagonist is thus a microcosm of volumes 5 and 6 of the *Recherche:* the almost delirious and uncanny alternation between imprisonment and escape. The efforts to imprison, as we later learn in *La Fugitive,* are doomed to failure, and true knowledge of Albertine's wayward activities comes in an ironical series of retrospective telegrams and messages. To the reader aware of the ultimate outcome of the couple's liaison, it seems impossible not to conclude that those moments of repose in which Marcel "possesses" Albertine are in fact the result of extreme delusion. The prisoner is forever a fugitive, and the poetic beauty of the passage describing her as primitive inanimate vegetal life arises from an active forgetfulness, or strong repression.

The progression of the text is toward a highly charged eroticism. The hero at first lies alongside the body of Albertine, listening to her breathing, then comes to sexual climax while she continues to sleep. This is satisfying to him above other forms of enjoyment because, in the narrator's words, "il me semblait à ces moments-là que je venais de la posséder plus complètement, comme une chose inconsciente et sans résistance de la muette nature." For our purposes, it is important to note as well that Albertine pronounces words, perhaps names of other people, as Marcel makes love to her, or rather, to himself. Yet these incoherent sounds do not bother him, since it is his hand and his body she touches. Masturbation *on* another human being whose maternal presence as sea and breath offers unmediated communion without the threat of sexual difference: this is, in Lacanian terms, identification with the mother's "phallus," the hero's desire being not to have, but to *be* the phallus. The entire passage leading up to the paragraph on naming can be interpreted in a Lacanian vein, as an elaborate *mise en scène* of the "imaginaire," where intersubjective relationships never get beyond the vicious circle of continuously vacillating symmetrical opposites. Some eighty pages later, when the name "Marcel" is mentioned for the second and last time in the novel, it is in the context of a discussion of the master-slave duality that characterizes Marcel's life with Albertine. In a moment of aphoristic lucidity, the narrator admits: "J'étais plus maître que je n'avais cru. Plus maître, c'est-à-dire plus esclave."

A presumed mastery is the mask for slavery, but what is the significance of *masking* as such? We can best understand the generalized paradigm underlying an apparently sexual combat in the guise of "jealousy" if we remember that Albertine is, among other things, a text. She is a "bloc-notes" whose lies must be deciphered "à rebours." The ironical thrust of the passage under scrutiny resides in the false affirmation, on the most evident thematic level, that Marcel is Albertine's "master" also in the sense of "teacher" or initiator into the secrets of the beaux-arts. The allegorical level of the text deconstructs this literal level, revealing the monstrosity of the narrator's claim to master a text that is, by definition, the very essence of Proustian "fuite." The allegory of the text *as* text demonstrates the peculiar *tourniquet* that characterizes the act of reading: a movement of simultaneous affirmation and denial in which the meanings of the sign can never preclude the violent moment of semantic appropriation.

The erotic pleasure experienced by Marcel in the earlier part of the passage merges eventually into a general feeling of possessive power as Albertine makes her transition from sleep to wakefulness. For the protagonist-jailer (reader) it is gratifying to know that the imprisoned woman (text) comes to life within the confining walls of his own domain. The movement from unconsciousness or *vertige* to *certitude* will be recognized as a structural repetition of the novel's "Overture," in which the protagonist's acts of remembering emerge from the chaos of remembered time. In *La Prisonnière,* the duality narrator-protagonist ("das errinernde ich" and "das erinnerte ich") is replaced by the couple of Marcel and Albertine, but the very same question of the text's ultimate readability is at stake in both cases. If we superimpose the later version of Albertine's coming-to-consciousness upon the first pages of the *Recherche,* we note an important and disquieting fact: for the (Hegelian) synthesis to take place, the narrator must "imprison" the protagonist as Marcel imprisons Albertine, by limiting the proliferation of his potential significance. Granted the structural equivalence:

$$\frac{\text{das erinnernde ich}}{\text{das erinnerte ich}} : \frac{\text{Marcel}}{\text{Albertine}}$$

the text then opens into deep irony. The apparent relationship of metaphorical synecdoche between narrator and protagonist collapses into pure metonymy or chance juxtaposition. According to this equivalence, the narrator "touches" the protagonist as Marcel lies *on* Albertine—for narcissistic gratification, without penetration or sharing of "essence." A simultaneous rereading of both passages shows that the "Eve" born of Marcel's thigh in the "Overture" is a model for Albertine as sex object: "Quelquefois, comme Eve naquit d'une côte d'Adam, une femme naissait pendant mon sommeil d'une fausse position de ma cuisse. Formée du plaisir que j'étais sur le point de goûter, je m'imaginais que c'était elle qui me l'offrait." The two passages undermine each other. On the one hand, the relationship between Marcel and Albertine is revealed as the false dialogue of a self-loving subject; and on the other hand, the posited unity of the two "I"'s becomes the vicious cycle of an eternal dialogue in which the point of contact between narrator and protagonist is nothing more than the imaginary space of a coincidence.

The final, most destructive irony of the text, emerges in Albertine's words at the moment of her awakening: "Elle retrouvait la parole, elle disait: 'Mon' ou 'Mon chéri,' suivis l'un ou l'autre de mon nom de baptême, ce qui, en donnant au narrateur le même prénom qu'à l'auteur de ce livre, eût fait: 'Mon Marcel,' 'Mon chéri Marcel.' " In allegorical terms, the subject who thought to possess the *other* as object, is dispossessed in the very instant of his naming. Indeed, the narrator possesses nothing, since his name, derived hypothetically from that of the author, is produced or proffered by a purely fictional character. And since Albertine stands for the elusive temporality of the sign, we find, through another structural substitution, that the reader, thinking to control meanings, is "read" by the text. The Freudian resonance of the passage as a unit is clear: the effort to deny the castration complex in a prolonged dream of narcissistic self-satisfaction collapses as the differences of the text explode to split the ego's claim to mastery.

The "autobiography" of Proust's *Recherche* is not to be understood in the literality of etymology as a "coming alive to oneself in writing," but rather, as the textual differential movement by which the "I" is separated from itself and thrust from the stability of discursive control into the alienating repetitions of the narrative's all-encompassing, *self-obliterating* rule. Narrative allegory, the temporal displacement of hypothetical fictions, emerges from the deconstruction of the empirical self's attempts to take possession of the text's body.

This *impossibility* of possession-taking has appeared under various guises and in differing forms of completion and complexity in the preceding pages. Swann's misreading of tropological nothingness was narrated as a subject's desire to embrace the personified "feminine" charms of the *petite phrase:* Swann wished to grasp that which is, by its very nature, a creature of *fuite* and elusiveness. The Ruskinian/Romantic pattern of possession-taking was taken over by Proust and used primarily as a semiological investigation: the "essence" of the outside world, whether incorporated in the aesthetic mysteries of music, the appeal of magic names, or the enigmatic significance of *Jeunes filles en fleurs,* is clothed in the form of the romantic symbol and expressed as a dream of plenitude whose false premises are revealed at every step of the *Recherche's* disillusioning path. Proust's novel is, among other things, a search for essences or truths, but the narrative deployment of the quest itself takes place within the constitutive splits of the sign. The travel motif, which had been associated only with the ecstasies of artistic revelation in Ruskin's *Praeterita,* becomes, for Proust, the most adequate fictional vehicle to depict the inner movement of negative self-discovery. The turn inward, which corresponds to the adoption of an abstract allegorical narration, yields the anguished, "jealous" investigations of the lover/reader in search of an absent, invisible, or undecipherable beloved/sign.

Confessional autobiography is the constantly repeated erroneous moment of subjective delusions whose "unravelling" in allegory produces a uniform subcurrent of irony. The reassuring appearance of authorial identity in the word "Marcel" is a disguise for the fact that the name, by its very insertion in fiction, loses all "necessary" or "essential" significant ties to the outside world. The congruence of the fictional "Marcel" with Marcel Proust is the deceptive effect of a purely contingent coincidence. Yet the *Recherche* thrives on such deception, and it is impossible for the reader not to participate in the text's referential illusion. Reading, for Proust, involved two mutually contradictory postulations: the movement of appropriation whereby the self, in its efforts to embrace the meaning of textual events, extends beyond the confines of its subjective prison in its search for referential verification (autobiography); and the cycle of dispossession whereby the self's stability is undermined by the disseminated multiplicity of unreadable signs (fictional allegory). The *Recherche* is the space in which these opposing constellations collide, the imaginary locus of the reader's impossible choices.

Chronology

1871   Marcel Proust is born on July 10 in Auteuil to Doctor Adrien Proust, the son of a grocer from Illiers, and Jeanne Weil Proust, the daughter of a wealthy Jewish stockbroker. The family lives in Paris and spends summers in Illiers.

1873   On May 24 Robert Proust, Marcel Proust's younger brother, is born.

1879   Proust plays with Marie and Nelly Benardaky in the Champs Elysées. Marie is presumably an early model for Gilberte.

1880   Proust has his first asthma attack.

1882–89   At the Lycée Condorcet, Proust studies with the philosopher Alphonse Darlu, who has a profound and permanent influence on him. He begins visiting the fashionable salon of Mme. Straus, the mother of one of his schoolfellows. He also makes the acquaintance of Laure Hayman, a celebrated courtesan, who probably contributed much to Proust's portrait of Odette.

1889–90   Proust joins the army and is sent to Orléans for his year of military service, where he meets Robert de Billy, who is probably the model for aspects of Robert de Saint-Loup. He also meets Anatole France in a fashionable salon.

1893   Proust meets Robert de Montesquiou, who sees that Proust is invited to the most exclusive salons. Montesquiou also suggests to him many aspects of the Baron de Charlus. In the fall, Proust receives a law degree from the École libre des sciences politiques.

1895   Proust receives a degree in literature and is hired by the Bibliothèque Mazarine, but leaves immediately in order to travel with the composer Reynaldo Hahn.

1895–99	Proust works on *Jean Santeuil,* which is not published until 1952, well after the author's death. Usually considered an initial draft of *A la recherche du temps perdu, Jean Santeuil* is, however, more directly autobiographical.
1896	Proust publishes *Les Plaisirs et les jours,* a collection of prose pieces mostly written between 1892 and 1893. The book is illustrated by Madeleine Lemaire and introduced by Anatole France.
1898	During the Dreyfus Affair, Proust's passionate support of Dreyfus puts a strain on many of his relationships in society.
1899	Proust begins translating Ruskin. His English is very poor but his mother, anxious that he commit himself to his literary work, helps him. Proust's asthmatic condition has worsened considerably.
1900	Proust travels to Venice with his mother in May; he takes another trip there in October.
1902	After traveling around France for most of the year, Proust visits Holland.
1903	Proust's father dies on November 26.
1904	Proust publishes his translation of Ruskin's *Bible of Amiens.*
1905	Proust's mother dies on September 26.
1905–6	Proust spends six months in a sanitorium. He continues to translate Ruskin. He moves to 102 boulevard Haussmann in Paris.
1907	Proust travels by car through Normandy. Alfred Agostinelli, who was in many respects Proust's model for Albertine, is his chauffeur.
1908	Proust begins some sketches for *A la recherche du temps perdu,* and starts working on *Contre Sainte-Beuve.*
1909–10	Proust finishes *Contre Sainte-Beuve* but has trouble finding a publisher. In 1910, he has the walls of his bedroom lined with cork for soundproofing.
1913	Bernard Grasset agrees to publish Proust's novel, which he has been writing almost continuously since 1908, at the author's expense. *Du côté de chez Swann* appears on November 13. In November, Alfred Agostinelli leaves Proust to go to the Côte d'Azur. The "fugitive" takes up aviation and dies in a plane crash on May 30, 1914.

1914–19   Proust leads a secluded existence and works on his novel. The Nouvelle Revue Française has taken over the publishing of Proust's work, and produces *A l'ombre des jeunes filles en fleurs* in November 1918. This volume receives the Prix Goncourt in December 1919, when the N.R.F. also publishes *Pastiches et mélanges*. Proust is forced to move out of his apartment; he moves to 44 rue Hamelin.

1920   *Le Côté de Guermantes I*, *Le Côté de Guermantes II*, and *Sodome et Gomorrhe I* published by the N.R.F.

1922   *Sodome et Gomorrhe II* published. On November 18 Proust dies of pneumonia.

1923   *La Prisonnière* published.

1925   *Albertine disparue* published.

1927   *Le Temps retrouvé* published.

Contributors

HAROLD BLOOM, Sterling Professor of the Humanities at Yale University, is the author of *The Anxiety of Influence, Poetry and Repression,* and many other volumes of literary criticism. His forthcoming study, *Freud: Transference and Authority,* attempts a full-scale reading of all of Freud's major writings. A MacArthur Prize Fellow, he is general editor of five series of literary criticism published by Chelsea House.

SAMUEL BECKETT is one of the most important contemporary figures in literature. Best known for his plays such as *Waiting for Godot, Krapp's Last Tape,* and *Happy Days,* he is also the author of stories, novels, and poetry. Born in Ireland, he has lived most of his adult life in France.

WALTER BENJAMIN, who committed suicide at the beginning of World War II, was Germany's foremost literary critic of this century. *Illuminations* is his best known work in English. Two of his other major works available in English are *Charles Baudelaire: A Lyric Poet in the Era of High Capitalism* and *The Origin of German Tragic Drama.*

GEORGES BATAILLE, who died in 1962, was a French poet, novelist, and philosopher. He founded, in 1946, the journal *Critique,* one of the most influential of the postwar period. In addition to *Literature and Evil* he was the author of *The Story of the Eye, Lascaux: Or, the Birth of Art,* and *Death and Sensuality: A Study of Eroticism and the Taboo.*

RENÉ GIRARD is Andrew B. Hammond Professor of French Language, Literature, and Civilization at Stanford University. In addition to *Deceit, Desire, and the Novel* his other major work available in English is *Violence and the Sacred.*

RICHARD MACKSEY is Professor of Humanities at The Johns Hopkins University. He is co-editor of *The Structuralist Controversy: The Lan-*

guages of Criticism and *The Sciences of Man,* and he is the author of articles on Proust, Ruskin, and Keats.

GEORGES POULET was a leading member of the Geneva school of criticism. Among his works available in English are *The Metamorphoses of the Circle, The Interior Distance,* and *Studies in Human Time.*

PAUL DE MAN was, until his death in 1983, Sterling Professor of Comparative Literature at Yale University. He is the author of *Blindness and Insight: Essays in Contemporary Criticism, Allegories of Reading: Figural Language in Rousseau, Nietzsche, Rilke, and Proust,* and *The Rhetoric of Romanticism,* and of the forthcoming collections, *The Resistance of Theory, Aesthetic Ideology,* and *Fugitive Essays.*

RICHARD TERDIMAN teaches literature at the University of California at San Diego. In addition to *The Dialectics of Isolation* he is the author of *Discourse/Counter-Discourse: The Theory and Practice of Symbolic Resistance in Nineteenth-Century France.*

DAVID R. ELLISON is Dean of Studies at Mount Holyoke College. *The Reading of Proust* is his first book.

Bibliography

Adam International Review 25, no. 260 (1957). "Marcel Proust: A World Symposium."

Albaret, Céleste. *Monsieur Proust*. Edited by Georges Belmont, translated by Barbara Bray. New York: McGraw-Hill, 1976.

Atget, Eugène. *A Vision of Paris: The Words of Marcel Proust*. Edited and introduced by Arthur A. Trottenberg. New York: Macmillan, 1980.

Barker, Richard Hindry. *Marcel Proust: A Biography*. New York: Criterion Books, 1958.

Barthes, Roland, et al. *Recherche de Proust*. Paris: Éditions du Seuil, 1980.

Bell, Clive. *Proust*. London: The Hogarth Press, 1928.

Bell, William Stewart. *Proust's Nocturnal Muse*. New York: Columbia University Press, 1962.

Benoist-Méchin, Jacques Gabriel Paul Michel. *Avec Marcel Proust*. Paris: A. Michel, 1977.

Bersani, Jacques, ed. *Les Critiques de notre temps et Proust*. Paris: Garnier, 1971.

Bersani, Leo. *Marcel Proust: The Fictions of Life and of Art*. New York: Oxford University Press, 1965.

Brée, Germaine. *Marcel Proust and Deliverance from Time*. Translated by C. J. Richards and A. D. Truitt. New Brunswick, N.J.: Rutgers University Press, 1955.

———. *The World of Marcel Proust*. Boston: Houghton Mifflin, 1966.

Bucknall, Barbara J. *The Religion of Art in Proust*. Urbana: University of Illinois Press, 1969.

Casey, Edward S. "Literary Description and Phenomenological Method." *Yale French Studies*, no. 61 (1981): 176–201.

Cattaui, Georges. *Marcel Proust*. Translated by Ruth Hall. New York: Funk & Wagnalls, 1968.

Cocking, John Martin. *Proust*. New Haven: Yale University Press, 1956.

Coleman, Elliott. *The Golden Angel: Papers on Proust*. New York: C. Taylor, 1954.

Culler, Jonathan. "The Problem of Metaphor." In *Language, Meaning, and Style: Essays in Memory of Stephen Ullmann*, 5–20, edited by T. E. Hope, T. B. W. Reid, Roy Harris, and Glanville Price. Leeds: Leeds University Press, 1981.

Curtius, Ernst Robert. *Marcel Proust*. Translated into French by Armand Pierhal. Paris: La Revue Nouvelle, 1928.

de Billy, Robert. *Marcel Proust: Lettres et conversations*. Paris: Editions des portiques, 1930.

Deleuze, Gilles. *Proust and Signs*. Translated by Richard Howard. New York: Braziller, 1972.

Descombes, Vincent. "La Révélation de l'abîme." *Degrés* 26–27 (Spring–Summer 1981): c1–c15.

Doubrovsky, Serge. "The Place of the Madeleine: Writing and Phantasy in Proust." *Boundary 2* 3, no. 1 (Fall 1975): 107–34.

Ellis, Havelock. "Marcel Proust." *Atlantic Monthly* 156, no. 4 (Oct. 1935): 421–32.

L'Esprit Créateur 11, no. 1 (Spring 1971). "Marcel Proust (Anniversary Issue)."

Fernandez, Ramon. *Messages*. Translated by Montgomery Belgion. New York: Harcourt, Brace & World, 1927.

Festa-McCormick, Diana. *Proustian Optics of Clothes: Mirrors, Masks, Mores*. Saratoga, Calif.: Anma Libri, 1984.

Feuillerat, Albert. *Comment Marcel Proust a composé son roman*. New Haven: Yale University Press, 1934.

Forster, E. M. "Proust." In *Abinger Harvest*, 96–102. New York: Harcourt, Brace & World, 1964.

Fowlie, Wallace. *A Reading of Proust*. Garden City, N.Y.: Anchor Books, 1964.

Frank, Joseph. "Spatial Form in Modern Literature." In *The Widening Gyre*, 3–62. New Brunswick, N.J.: Rutgers University Press, 1963.

Genette, Gérard. "Time and Narrative in *A la recherche du temps perdu*." In *Aspects of Narrative: Selected Papers from the English Institute*, 93–118. Translated by Paul de Man, edited by J. Hillis Miller. New York: Columbia University Press, 1971.

Gide, André. *Journals, 1889–1949*. Selected, edited, and translated by Justin O'Brien. London: Pelican, 1967.

———. *Pretexts: Reflections on Literature and Morality*. Selected, edited, and translated by Justin O'Brien. London: Secker & Warburg, 1959.

Girard, René, ed. *Proust: A Collection of Critical Essays*. Englewood Cliffs, N.J.: Prentice-Hall, 1962.

Grossvogel, David I. "Proust: *Remembrance of Things Past*." In *Limits of the Novel: Evolutions of a Form from Chaucer to Robbe-Grillet*. Ithaca, N.Y.: Cornell University Press, 1968.

Hardy, Barbara. *Tellers and Listeners: The Narrative Imagination*. London: Athlone, 1975.

Hindus, Milton. *The Proustian Vision*. New York: Columbia University Press, 1954.

Houston, John Porter. *The Shape and Style of Proust's Novel*. Detroit: Wayne State University Press, 1982.

Hughes, Edward J. *Marcel Proust: A Study in the Quality of Awareness*. New York: Cambridge University Press, 1983.

Humphries, Jefferson. *The Otherness Within: Gnostic Readings in Marcel Proust, Flannery O'Connor, and François Villon*. Baton Rouge, La.: Louisiana State University Press, 1983.

Jay, Paul. "Joyce and Proust: The Theory of Fictional Autobiography." In *Being in the Text: Self-Representation from Wordsworth to Roland Barthes*, 142–53. Ithaca, N.Y.: Cornell University Press, 1984.

Jephcott, E. F. N. *Proust and Rilke: The Literature of Expanded Consciousness*. New York: Barnes & Noble, 1972.

Johnson, J. Theodore. "Proust's 'Impressionism' Reconsidered in the Light of the Visual Arts of the Twentieth Century." In *Twentieth-Century French Fiction: Essays for Germaine Brée*, 27–56. Edited by George Stambolian. New Brunswick, N.J.: Rutgers University Press, 1975.

Joiner, Lawrence D. *The Art of the Proustian Novel Reconsidered*. Rock Hill, S.C.: Winthrop College, 1979.

Kamber, Gerald, and Richard Macksey. " 'Negative Metaphor' and Proust's Rhetoric of Absence." *MLN* 85, no. 6 (Dec. 1970): 858–83.

Kassell, Walter. *Marcel Proust and the Strategy of Reading*. Philadelphia: J. Benjamins, 1980.

Kilmartin, Terence. *A Reader's Guide to* Remembrance of Things Past. New York: Random House, 1983.

Kopp, Richard L. *Marcel Proust as a Social Critic*. Rutherford, N.J.: Fairleigh Dickinson University Press, 1971.

Ladimer, Bethany. "The Narrator as Voyeur in *A la recherche du temps perdu*." *Critical Quarterly* 19, no. 3 (Autumn 1977): 5–20.

Levin, Harry. *The Gates of Horn: A Study of Five French Realists*. New York: Oxford University Press, 1963.

March, Harold. *The Two Worlds of Marcel Proust*. 1948. Reprint. New York: Russell & Russell, 1968.

Mauriac, François. *Proust's Way*. Translated by Elsie Pell. New York: Philosophical Library, 1950.

Maurois, André. *Proust: Portrait of a Genius*. Translated by Gerard Hopkins. New York: Harper, 1950.

————. *The World of Marcel Proust*. Translated by Maura Budberg with the assistance of Barbara Creed. New York: Harper & Row, 1974.

May, Derwent. *Proust*. New York: Oxford University Press, 1983.

Mehlman, Jeffrey. *A Structural Study of Autobiography: Proust, Leiris, Sartre, Lévi-Strauss*. Ithaca, N.Y.: Cornell University Press, 1974.

Melnick, Daniel. "Proust, Music, and the Reader." *Modern Language Quarterly* 41, no. 2 (June 1980): 181–92.

Moss, Howard. *The Magic Lantern of Marcel Proust: A Critical Study of* Remembrance of Things Past. Boston: Nonpareil Books, 1963.

Murray, Jack. *The Proustian Comedy*. York, S.C.: French Literature Publications, 1980.

Nordlinger-Reifstahl, Marie. "Proust as I Knew Him." *London Magazine* 1, no. 7 (August 1954): 51–61.

Ortega y Gasset, José. "Time, Distance, and Form in Proust." Translated by I. Singer. *The Hudson Review* 11, no. 4 (Winter 1958): 504–13.

Painter, George D. *Proust*. 2 vols. Boston: Little, Brown, 1959–65.

Peyre, Henri. *Marcel Proust*. New York: Columbia University Press, 1970.

Pinter, Harold. *The Proust Screenplay*. London: Eyre-Methuen, 1978.

Poulet, Georges. *Proustian Space*. Translated by Elliott Coleman. Baltimore: Johns Hopkins University Press, 1977.

Price, Larkin B., ed. *Marcel Proust: A Critical Panorama*. Urbana: University of Illinois Press, 1973.

Proust, Marcel. *Letters of Marcel Proust to Antoine Bibesco*. Translated by Gerard Hopkins, London: Thames & Hudson, 1953.

————. *Marcel Proust: Selected Letters, 1880–1903*. Edited by Philip Kolb, translated by Ralph Manheim. Garden City, N.Y.: Doubleday, 1983.

Quennell, Peter, ed. *Marcel Proust, 1871–1922: A Centennial Volume*. New York: Simon & Schuster, 1971.

Revel, Jean François. *On Proust*. Translated by Martin Turnell. New York: Library Press, 1972.

Ricardou, Jean. "Proust: A Retrospective Reading." Translated by Erica Freiberg. *Critical Inquiry* 8, no. 3 (Spring 1982): 531–41.

Riffaterre, Michael. "Descriptive Imagery." *Yale French Studies*, no. 61 (1981): 107–25.

Rivers, J. E. *Proust and the Art of Love: The Aesthetics of Sexuality in the Life, Times, and Art of Marcel Proust*. New York: Columbia University Press, 1981.

Sansom, William. *Proust and His World*. London: Thames & Hudson, 1973.

Schehr, Lawrence R. "Proust's Musical Inversions." *MLN* 97, no. 5 (Dec. 1982): 1086–99.

Scott-Moncrieff, Charles Kenneth, ed. *Marcel Proust: An English Tribute*. London: Chatto & Windus, 1923.

Shattuck, Roger. *Marcel Proust*. Princeton, N.J.: Princeton University Press, 1982.

————. *Proust's Binoculars: A Study of Memory, Time, and Recognition in A la recherche du temps perdu*. New York: Random House, 1963.

Slater, Maya. *Humor in the Works of Proust*. New York: Oxford University Press, 1979.

Spalding, Philip Anthony. *A Reader's Handbook to Proust: An Index Guide to Remembrance of Things Past*. Rev. ed., revised by R. H. Cortie. New York: Barnes & Noble, 1975.

Splitter, Randolph. "Proust, Joyce, and the Theory of Metaphor." *Literature and Psychology* 29, nos. 1 and 2 (1979): 4–17.

————. *Proust's Recherche: A Psychoanalytic Interpretation*. Boston: Routledge & Kegan Paul, 1981.

Stambolian, George. *Marcel Proust and the Creative Encounter*. Chicago: University of Chicago Press, 1972.

Taylor, Elisabeth Russell. *Marcel Proust and His Contexts: A Critical Bibliography of English Language Scholarship*. New York: Garland, 1981.

Taylor, Rosalie. "The Adult World and Childhood in *Combray*." *French Studies* 22, no. 1 (Jan. 1968): 26–36.

Ullmann, Stephen. "The Metaphorical Texture of a Proustian Novel." In *The Image in the Modern French Novel: Gide, Alain-Fournier, Proust, Camus*, 124–238. Cambridge: Cambridge University Press, 1960.

————. "Transpositions of Sensations in Proust's Imagery." In *Style in the French Novel*, 189–209. Cambridge: Cambridge University Press, 1960.

Vigneron, Robert. "Structure de *Swann*." *Modern Philology* 45 (1948): 185–207.

Wharton, Edith. "Marcel Proust." *Yale Review* 14, no. 2 (Jan. 1925): 209–22.

Wilson, Edmund. "Marcel Proust." In *Axel's Castle*, 132–90. New York: Scribner's, 1931.

Woolf, Virginia. "Phases of Fiction." In *Granite and Rainbow*, 93–145. New York: Harcourt, Brace & World, 1958.

Yale French Studies, no. 34 (June 1965). "Proust."

Zimmerman, Eugenia N. "Death and Transfiguration in Proust and Tolstoy." *Mosaic* 6, no. 2 (Winter 1973): 161–72.

———. "The Metamorphoses of Adam: Names and Things in Sartre and Proust." In *Twentieth-Century French Fiction: Essays for Germaine Brée,* edited by George Stambolian, 57–71. New Brunswick, N.J.: Rutgers University Press.

Acknowledgments

"Memory, Habit, Time" (originally untitled) by Samuel Beckett from *Proust* by Samuel Beckett, © 1957 by Samuel Beckett. Reprinted by permission of Grove Press, Inc., and John Calder Ltd.

"The Image of Proust" by Walter Benjamin from *Illuminations*, edited by Hannah Arendt and translated by Harry Zohn, © 1955 by Suhrkamp Verlag, English translation © 1968 by Harcourt, Brace & World. Reprinted by permission of Harcourt Brace Jovanovich, Inc.

"Proust and Evil" (originally entitled "Proust") by Georges Bataille from *Literature and Evil* by Georges Bataille, © 1957 by Editions Gallimard, English translation © 1973 by Calder & Boyars Ltd. Reprinted by permission. This essay originally appeared in *La littérature et le mal* (Editions Gallimard, 1957).

"The Worlds of Proust" by René Girard from *Deceit, Desire, and the Novel: Self and Other in Literary Structure* by René Girard, © 1961 by Editions Bernard Grasset, English translation © 1965 by the Johns Hopkins University Press, Baltimore/London. Reprinted by permission. This essay originally appeared in *Mensonge romantique et vérité romanesque* (Editions Bernard Grasset, 1961).

"The Architecture of Time: Dialectics and Structure" by Richard Macksey from *Proust: A Collection of Critical Essays*, edited by René Girard, © 1962 by Prentice-Hall, Inc., Englewood Cliffs, New Jersey. Reprinted by permission.

"Proustian Space" (originally untitled) by Georges Poulet from *Proustian Space* by Georges Poulet, © 1963 by Editions Gallimard, English translation © 1977 by the Johns Hopkins University Press, Baltimore/London. Reprinted by permission. This essay originally appeared in *L'Espace proustien* (Editions Gallimard, 1963).

"Reading (Proust)" by Paul de Man from *Allegories of Reading: Figural Language in Rousseau, Nietzsche, Rilke, and Proust* by Paul de Man, © 1979 by Yale University. Reprinted by permission of Yale University Press. This essay originally appeared as "Proust et l'allégorie de la lecture" in *Mouvements premiers: Etudes critiques offertes à Georges Poulet* (Librarie José Carti, 1972).

"The Depreciation of the Event" by Richard Terdiman from *The Dialectics of Isolation: Self and Society in the French Novel from the Realists to Proust* by

Richard Terdiman, © 1976 by Yale University. Reprinted by permission of Yale University Press.

"The Self in/as Writing" by David R. Ellison from *The Reading of Proust* by David R. Ellison, © 1984 by the Johns Hopkins University Press, Baltimore/London. Reprinted by permission.

Index